reclaiming
family time

—— A GUIDE TO ——

SLOWING DOWN AND SAVORING

THE GIFT OF ONE ANOTHER

reclaiming family time

A GUIDE TO

SLOWING DOWN AND SAVORING

THE GIFT OF ONE ANOTHER

TIM AND SUE MULDOON

Published by The Word Among Us Press

7115 Guilford Drive, Suite 100

Frederick, Maryland 21704

wau.org

21 20 19 18 17   1 2 3 4 5

ISBN: 978-1-59325-313-4

eISBN: 978-1-59325-495-7

Cover design by Faceout Studios

Made and printed in the United States of America

Library of Congress Control Number: 2017946606

Love needs time and space; everything else is secondary. Time is needed to talk things over, to embrace leisurely, to share plans, to listen to one other and gaze in each other's eyes, to appreciate one another and to build a stronger relationship. Sometimes the frenetic pace of our society and the pressures of the workplace create problems. At other times, the problem is the lack of quality time together, sharing the same room without one even noticing the other.

—Pope Francis, *Amoris Laetitia*

Contents

Losing Family Time

I f you are a parent—and we suspect you are, if you've picked up this book—then you probably are like us, in the sense of constantly asking how to reclaim family time. First of all, congrats on carving out some time to give that question some thought. We are convinced that it is an important part of relishing our busy lives with children.

You probably intuit on some level that the deck is stacked against us, that something in our modern culture tends to make family life extraordinarily difficult, even compared to the modern culture from which we are removed by less than a generation. You sense that there are social forces that tend to pull us away from each other and demand of us more running around just to keep up. You find yourself stressed and low on sleep. You crave some down time. You worry about whether you have the right priorities. You are concerned about how all this busyness affects your children and long for an opportunity to (a) make it stop and (b) not have your kids freak out.

This book asks some big questions and offers you the chance to reflect on how you choose to answer them. It will not provide easy answers, because we are convinced that parents are the only ones who can understand the specific challenges that face their families. It will point to factors in our culture that compromise family time in ways that are unprecedented and that thus put parents in the position of having to choose how much to go along and how much to hold back, even in the face of their children's complaints.

We see clues to these cultural factors whenever we slow down long enough to talk about the family calendar for the coming month. We are the parents of three teens: two girls and a boy, all socially active young people. Our oldest is, at this writing, on the verge of getting a driver's license, but for now that observation implies that we are still responsible for getting her and her siblings everywhere they need to go. We must plan work schedules, school schedules, after-school sports and activities, weekend sports and activities, time out with friends, and—oh yes, because of reasons we'll explain later—time to get to church.

> What we've observed in our fast-paced, high-octane world is a tendency to take on too much, both for ourselves and our families.

Our family life is centripetal, to use an image from a high school physics class; it is constantly spinning, throwing each of its members out into the world like a blender that has lost its lid. There is, of course, a strong temptation to hit the off button, and occasionally we do—on holidays, for example. But we find that too much control over our kids' time can cause resentment, an attitude that can be corrosive for family life. So we often wonder how we might walk the fine line between positive social engagement, on the one hand, and a strong family life, on the other.

In the process of sorting this out, we have taken a close look at what has become the new normal for planning kids' activities. Recently we were on the soccer field after one of our children had finished up a game. We were chatting with another parent who, at ten in the morning, was already looking exhausted. "What are you all up to this weekend?" Sue asked. The woman sighed and talked about how many activities were still planned for the day. "Ben has two baseball games and a lacrosse game; Julia has a soccer game and then her chorus concert." Our friend had something of a disbelieving look on her own face as she said these things, wondering (we thought) why in the world she had ever packed her average weekend schedule so tightly.

That conversation, and many others like it (often on the sidelines of one of our kids' sporting events), has led us to think about the ways we schedule our time and budget our money. We too feel harried; we too sometimes spend hours on the road, schlepping from school to friends' houses to various activities to work and so on. We too have missed dinners as a family, done work late into the night, spent long holiday weekends at soccer or basketball tournaments, and found ourselves losing sleep at night. Eventually, we asked a simple question: why?

Time Crunch

What we've observed in our fast-paced, high-octane world is a tendency to take on too much, both for ourselves and our families. We see it in our own tendencies sometimes, and we'll talk about some of our own challenges in this book. But we also see it in our professional lives. We see young people who have high levels of stress and who, studies show, are more likely to exhibit anxiety than in prior generations. We see parents who have no lives for themselves and no time to spend on building their marriages because they are constantly getting their kids to their activities. We see families who prioritize their kids' social lives, especially through sports, to the extent that they have no time for fun, no time for sabbath rest, no time to pray. We see parents who take vacations with their families but come back exhausted because they need vacations even from their vacations. What is going on here?

When we first mentioned to Sue's mom that we were writing a book on reclaiming family life from overscheduling, she stifled a laugh. God love her, she didn't say it out loud—but she was thinking, "Who are you people to be writing about overscheduling?" She sees our busy lives on a daily basis. For the past twelve years, most of our older children's lives, we've lived in a town outside of Boston where it seems all parents expect their children to be academic, athletic, and artistic all-stars. Shuttling kids to activities is part of parents' routines, both moms and dads. Conversations on the sidelines or during stage prep are about which kid is doing what activity next season, what camps kids are signed up for, and my, how busy we all are!

Ours is a place of standardized-test preparation, academic camps in every subject over the summer, regional club sports leagues for kids as young as six (because, you know, college scholarships), music and theater productions, and more. We've gotten up at 4 a.m. to register our kids for swim lessons. We've camped out in front of multiple computer screens in order to make sure our daughter got into the local theater production as soon as they opened online sign-ups. We've attended chorus concerts, band concerts, Christmas pageants, and school drama productions and, of course, blocked off entire weekends for soccer tournaments.

We're out the door by 6:55 a.m. and driving kids to schools in different towns. (At our worst, it was three schools in three different towns.) Later in the day, we're juggling trips to friends' houses, soccer fields, or basketball courts. We're juggling who will make dinner, how many people will make it, and what activities are happening later in the evening or over the weekend. We try to plan grocery shopping (sometimes), doing chores, keeping up with the house, taking care of the dog, and getting everyone to the doctor or dentist. Depending on the season, we try to get out Christmas cards, plan a New Year's party, celebrate Chinese New Year (since our kids are all from China) or St. Patrick's Day (since we grown-ups are Irish American), get together with family for Easter, rejoice with friends or family around graduations or confirmations, plan a summer vacation, or prepare for the start of the school year. We try to balance the budget, do the usual maintenance on our cars, keep the house and yard clean, help our neighbor down the street, participate in activities in school and church, and spend fun time with our children. Our lives are driven by to-do lists, and often we can barely keep up.

One of the clues to the way that contemporary American society has become overwhelmed is in our collective lack of sleep. Researchers are discovering more about the causes and effects of sleep loss, for both adults and children, and the news is alarming. Sleep loss is like jet lag: we carry its effects into daily life and often lack the time to recover from it. Chronic sleep debt is like "social jet lag," which can slow concentration and harm natural bodily systems.[1] In children, it may appear as attention deficit/hyperactivity disorder (ADHD) and may put them at risk for diabetes and obesity.[2] As a society, we are getting less sleep than even a few decades ago, perhaps because technology has made it easy to interrupt the usual circadian rhythms of the body.

Our aim is to speak to parents who want to practice a certain resistance to a frenetic culture with its sometimes-misguided values.

In our experience, part of the blame lies with schools: early start times and even homework expectations can crowd out opportunities for sleep.[3] One viral video from a second-grade teacher in Texas, for example, was about a no-homework policy meant to encourage more sleep and time with family; many people resonated with her questioning the assumption that more work equaled better performance. But there are other pressures as well: after-school sports and activities. We see many parents (ourselves included, sometimes) who have not found a good balance in the activities that their children engage in.

There has been a good deal of study of the question of whether kids are overscheduled. Bruce Feiler points to this research in his article "Overscheduled Children: How Big a Problem?"[4] He points to a number of books in recent years that have raised this question and reflects on his family's tendencies to crowd their schedule with activities. But he also notes that sometimes scheduled activities can be positive. He quotes Alvin Rosenfeld, a child and adolescent psychiatrist and one of the authors of *The Over-Scheduled Child*. Rosenfeld likens children's brains to a computer: "The basic idea is that it's great to have a computer, it's great to have software, but if you overload a computer with software it breaks down." Scheduled activities provide children with software—that is, experiences that offer them opportunities to learn and grow— but they have limits. Parents do too, and they must find a happy medium of fruitful experience and adequate rest.

Our rule of thumb tends to be that no child can be involved in more than one sport and perhaps one other organized activity during a given stretch of time. We always have an eye to schedule conflicts too, so that the question of choosing activities for each child is always at the same time a question about how that activity will impact our family life as a whole, especially as a result of all the time spent driving around.

Making Choices

We'll say more about certain parenting strategies in this book, but we begin with these observations to highlight the fact that in many ways, we haven't quite figured out how to reclaim family time from the busyness of modern life. So why did we say yes to writing this book? Because we wanted to spend some time discerning the question of how we prioritize family life. We consider ourselves somewhere in the middle of the scale of busy. We still make time for certain things like family dinner and going to Mass. Unlike many of our peers, we've chosen careers and made other life choices that really allow for making family life our central concern. But we too wonder about the big picture and whether our customary pace may get in the way of prioritizing what is most important in life.

We come at this question of scheduling from two very different angles, which we hope will overlap more and more: the practical, everyday side and the more idealistic, big-picture side. So first, a disclaimer: this is not a book that focuses only on the ideal. We are not monks, we are parents. And while we will draw a lesson or two from monastic spirituality, which might be described as a "spirituality of time," our aim is to speak to other parents like us: parents who want what's best for their kids and are willing to make sacrifices but who also want to practice a certain resistance to a frenetic culture with its sometimes-misguided values.

By describing our book as "a guide to slowing down and savoring the gift of one another," we are seeking perspective.

We'll unpack what that means in the coming pages by drawing from biblical resources that have for millennia focused people's attention on the imperative to keep God first in all things. But we'll also share some of the ordinary, everyday concerns that often make it hard for us to reach our ideals.

The bottom line is this: this is a book about encouraging prayerful discernment of the call to parenting. It does not propose a radical withdrawal from everyday concerns, nor does it propose an unrealistic countercultural model. It is neither an account of how we always get it right nor a how-to guide. Instead, it draws from the traditions of Christian spirituality as resources that help us as parents to listen daily to the voice of the Holy Spirit, even in the midst of busy lives, and to make wise choices that keep our priorities where they should be: on forming our families into communities rooted in faith and stretching toward the purposes for which God has created us.

What does discernment look like? A short answer is that it is grounded in the desire that all our choices flow from our lifelong conversation with God in prayer. So on a fundamental level, that means giving enough attention to our own prayer that it becomes a source of wise decision making. If you already pray regularly, this may seem obvious. However, if prayer is new to you, or if you are unsure how to establish a habit of prayer, then this book will give you some ideas on how to make it more central in your life. It will offer opportunities to pause and raise questions about yourself and your family life—opportunities that may spark conversations with your spouse or with friends in similar circumstances.

Some of the questions may evoke some soul-searching because they point us to the desires that often lie deep within our hearts and have their roots in the desires that God has for us. Offering these desires back to God is a simple, profound way that we can engage in prayer on a daily basis. You may find it helpful to journal or to discuss these questions with a friend or a book group. The point is to gain some perspective by taking a step back from your busy life to see the big picture.

At the end of every chapter, we'll pose questions for consideration or conversation with a spouse, friend, or book group. These will suggest practical steps for developing a more discerning attitude toward the way you prioritize time as a family. Below are some questions to get you started.

Questions for Discernment

1. Do you wish you had more time with your family? What are some things that get in the way?

2. Describe the factors that make it hard to reclaim family time. Which are necessary, and which are more optional?

3. What are some of the most life-giving ways you've spent time with your family? How have you created lasting memories?

4. Which of the activities that each of the members of your family engages in are most important? Which take the most time?

CHAPTER ONE

Work and Family

For what profit comes to mortals from all the toil and
anxiety of heart with which they toil under the sun?
Every day sorrow and grief are their occupation;
even at night their hearts are not at rest. This also is vanity.
—Ecclesiastes 2:22-23

The desire to serve the Lord in all things ought to be fundamental to who we are as followers of Jesus. Yet if you are like us, you get caught up in the small details that suck up our time and prevent us from seeing the big picture. For years, we've intuited that it's not just us—there are larger forces at work that impact the way we are able to manage our lives. So we did a little research, paying particular attention to the balance of work and family life that many Americans experience.

This chapter will pay particular attention to the situation of parents who work outside the home. In 2016, the US Department of Labor reported that over 60 percent of two-parent households had both parents working.[5] There are still a significant number of families in which one parent can work at home, but in our experience, those moms and dads are no less busy or committed to their work, whether domestic or professional.

There is an obvious trade-off that all parents understand: if you work, you are not spending time with your kids. If you are spending time with your kids, you are not working. And each of these choices comes with benefits and drawbacks, most especially around money. Those that have wealth can approach work differently: for them, the balance of work and family is a question for discernment rooted in a fundamental economic freedom. But for us, and for most people, that discernment has more the character of necessity. We are caught up in a larger economy that shapes the ways we can respond to that necessity.

> The call to family life involves sacrifice and the reorientation of priorities. It means having to rethink just about everything.

Brigid Schulte, the author of *Overwhelmed: Work, Love, and Play When No One Has the Time,* analyzes the social factors that contribute to the feeling she describes in the title. She notes that it is primarily parental work schedules that drive kids' activities and that the major change over recent decades has been about our attitudes toward work.[6] The onus has fallen particularly on women who, while entering the work force in large numbers, have nevertheless sought to spend more time with their children. According to sociologists Michael Hout and Caroline Hanley, in the late 1960s, only 38 percent of American mothers with young children worked outside the home, whereas in the early 2000s, that number had risen to 75 percent, with many mothers working full-time.

Working parents, they write, put in thirteen more hours per week at their workplaces in 2000 compared to 1970—amounting to a total of 676 hours or 28 days per year.[7] And ironically, during this same period mothers have spent more time with their children. Fathers are busy too: what was once leisure time is now devoted to children.[8]

Schulte raises important questions about the ways that the changing economic landscape in the United States over the past fifty years has impacted the way we use our time. If everyone is, to quote her title, "overwhelmed," how are we to respond? One answer, it would seem, would be to quit work and just spend time with family. Of course, not everyone could do that without going into financial crisis. Many families, it seems, do what we have done: make professional compromises in order to prioritize family life. Others compromise in the other directions, delaying or forgoing family life in order to focus on work.[9]

Work, Balance, and Family Time

If you are young, you may have opportunities to consider what kind of work life will be the best for raising a family.[10] We thought about that question early in our lives—and in fact, one of the attractions to education-related professions was that they offered more flexible schedules than some more high-pressure professions. But for many who have already made career decisions, the better question is how to negotiate the balance between the necessity of work and the desire for family life. From what we can see among friends, there is no clear answer, but there are certainly considerations that might foster a sense of growth in the right direction. One key question is this: do you consider work primarily as a means to care for your family, or are there fundamentally personal reasons that drive you to succeed at your work?

It can be difficult to reclaim family time. But what makes it possible, in our experience, is the embrace of the family vocation as a "pearl of great price."

Many parents we know choose to work, at least in part, because they like it, and because they believe in the work they are doing. Teachers, doctors, service professionals, and many others enjoy a sense of contributing to the world, which they see as both good for themselves personally and of benefit to their children. We remember comments from our kids to the effect that it would be great if we were doctors or lawyers— they perceived even at a young age that there was a benefit to having both social capital and more money!

There is a burgeoning field of the study of work-life balance, with university centers devoted to the subject.[11] Further, there is a more nuanced understanding of the various approaches parents take toward work. Researchers have identified at least six different approaches:

- Work: primarily oriented toward money making
- Career: advancing and testing yourself against others

- Passion: doing what you love
- Kinship: creating connections with others, as (for example) among firefighters
- Craftsmanship: doing something well for its own sake
- Service: doing something for the good of others[12]

In most of these orientations, the work itself has an intrinsic good beyond money, meaning that the person who approaches work through such a lens will not as easily feel the burnout that comes from what Studs Terkel called a "Monday through Friday kind of dying."

Parents can experience different orientations toward work over their lives, with some periods involving more than one. In our early adulthood, we both approached our work with a dominant service orientation: we hoped that the work we were doing did some good in the world. Our choices around work were rooted in a discernment of how our gifts might benefit people: Tim as a professor, Sue as a counselor. In many ways, we enjoyed our work and had a sense of direction and growth.

But when we adopted our first child, our predominant "service" orientation gave way to a much more fundamental sensibility that work was, well, *work*. We both would have preferred to stay home with our child; it was wrenching, especially early on, when we had to put her in day care in order to go to work. We needed the money. We know many, many families that have similarly wrestled with this decision driven by necessity. For us, the discernment process was not about *whether* to put her in day care; it was a question, rather, of *where* and for *how long.* In those years, with much prayer, we found placements on the campuses where we worked, and both of us found ways to flex our schedules in order to keep her hours in day care relatively short.

Do We Really Want to Reclaim Family Time?

Notice that all six approaches to work involve some balance between the desires a person has to make an impact in the world, on the one hand, and the desire to care for one's family. The difficult, important question for discernment is this: do I really want to reclaim family time? In other words, is reclaiming family time more important than whatever benefits I perceive from spending more time working?

Let's be honest with ourselves: building a career can be richly rewarding. It is good to make an impact, particularly in those professions that are oriented toward a common good. Devoting oneself to a passion, too, can be life-giving: we think of artists, for example, or those who have a deep love of teaching or healing. Similarly, those whose work is motivated by a deep care for those around them can be selfless and heroic; we think of family members who serve in law enforcement and the military, as well as others who are first responders and who develop a kind of family bond in their workplaces. And those who seek to produce beautiful crafts, whether acoustic guitars, beautiful furniture, or great novels, leave a piece of themselves in everything they produce. Work, in short, can be a deeply good use of one's talents, both for oneself and for the world.

Against that backdrop, it is more possible to understand why the call to family life is a deeply vocational call, one that involves sacrifice and the reorientation of priorities. The conscious embrace of that vocation means having to rethink just about everything: how we spend time and money, how we relate to other people, how we consider our roles in the community, how we vote, and so much more. Shifting one's priority away from work toward family is a fundamental reorientation of the self.

Women are in a particularly vulnerable situation, pressed to "have it all"— a rich professional life and a happy home life. That dream is just not realistic.

There was a period in our early family life, after we added a second child, when Sue was able to take time away from work. That decision was difficult because it did entail conversations about finances and the impact on Sue's professional life. We are very aware of how decisions around prioritizing family can often fall heavily on women. Brigid Schulte explores this issue in her book, wondering how women can grow in their careers if they need to take time away to care for children. She writes,

> What if you like your work, or at least some form of it? What if you can't quit your job or wouldn't know what to do with yourself on a farm? What if you can't afford help or if just scraping together your mortgage payment every month pretty much taps you out? Is dropping out really the only way out?[13]

She recognizes that many families (like ours) must make the decision whether to "drop out" of an economic system that makes it hard to balance family life and work life. We know a couple of families that have made such a decision: to live on a farm, practically off the grid, in order to avoid the pressures of needing to work simply to survive and leaving family life to the marginal evenings and weekends that are left over.

Schulte has a conversation with Kimberly Fisher, the secretary of the International Association for Time Use Research, to learn more about studies of women experiencing leisure. Noting that at times women's leisure was a reflection of their husband's social capital, Fisher suggests that historically, women entered religious life in order to escape having to enter the "laboring class."

In other words, religious life appears to her to be a way of dropping out of the usual dynamics that impact people's slavery to work. Leisure, she says, is for nuns. And while that explanation does not do justice to the discernment process, there is still a grain of truth in it. For it recognizes that religious life is about a fundamental reorientation of priorities and a refusal to be beholden to the imperative to make and spend money.

What Schulte and Fisher point to are economic conditions that impact nearly everyone who seeks to reclaim family time. Most of us, plainly speaking, are time crunched, and it's not always our fault. If you are trying to make ends meet by working, it's not possible to carve out many stress-free periods of family leisure. Schulte speaks to Lyn Craig, an Australian sociologist who studies women's time use, who concludes that women are in a particularly vulnerable situation, pressed to "have it all"—a rich professional life and a happy home life. That dream, she says, is not realistic.

> You can't have it all unless other things shift in other people's behavior—unless men actually reduce their working hours and increase their time doing housework and child care, unless cultures change and we're prepared to give social support to parents. Women have made all the changes unilaterally that they really can. I don't see what else they can do.[14]

Craig points to two related issues: the choices that men make and the cultural expectations that impact families. Both of these issues involve discernment, asking how our desires are shaped by the cultures in which we live and whether they lead us to greater or lesser joy. At times, we are convinced, it is necessary to make choices that run against the grain of others' expectations. For too often, those expectations are rooted in values other than those that contribute to the flourishing of family life or the building of God's kingdom.

Choosing the vocation to family life, then, can be countercultural. As parents, what we see when we look at American culture is remnants of a society oriented toward the family but which today appears more and more to prioritize competition, economic security, and the rule of technology. In short, it can be difficult to reclaim family time. But what makes it possible, in our experience, is the embrace of the family vocation as a "pearl of great price," a source of value that supersedes all other desires.

The Vocation to Family Life

In Christian tradition, a vocation is a way of living rooted in the understanding that the Lord has gifted us with talents that we are to put in service to his kingdom. Consider Paul's reflection on the various vocations within the Church:

> As a body is one though it has many parts, and all the parts of the body, though many, are one body, so also Christ. . . .
>
> Some people God has designated in the church to be, first, apostles; second, prophets; third, teachers; then, mighty deeds; then, gifts of healing, assistance, administration, and varieties of tongues. . . . Strive eagerly for the greatest spiritual gifts. (1 Corinthians 12:12, 28, 31)

Notice the way that Paul points to the different manifestations of God's gifts, all of which work together to build up Christ's body. Elsewhere he critiques attitudes that diminish the importance of some gifts: "The eye cannot say to the hand, 'I do not need you'" (1 Corinthians 12:21). The law of the Church, he suggests, is complementarity. What we see in contemporary society, on the contrary, is often a law of competition, one that has unfairly impacted women.

If a vocation is a living expression of fidelity to the God who has given us the gifts of our very selves, then there are as many vocations as there are people. Traditionally, the word *vocation* has referred to a particular form of lived discipleship: specifically, a particular form of the celibate, vowed life of nuns, priests, monks, or brothers. But the vocation to family life is another form of religious life, rooted in vows before God that call us to consecrate our families toward God's unfolding project in the world.

Today we encounter families in a variety of circumstances. We know priests who have been put in situations where they have had responsibility for raising a child—one through the death of a sibling, another through the adoption of an orphan without other choices. We know single men and women who have been moved to enter the adoption process, feeling called to give of themselves even in spite of a longtime desire to find a spouse. We have friends who are widows and widowers and who soldier on bravely after the death of a spouse and provide love and support to their children. We know people who have divorced and who still do everything they can to love their children and provide what they can. In all these cases, we see something of what Christ meant when he said that there is no greater love than the willingness to lay down one's life for a friend. Many parents lay down their lives for their children.

Those stories highlight for us anew what the call to marriage represents in the life of the Church: a call to partnership with another person whose complementary gifts offer children perspective on what it means to be a human being formed in the image of God. In recent decades, with changing attitudes toward marriage in modern societies, we can understand this approach to marriage in sharper contrast. Gone are the days when the path to marriage was practically a foregone conclusion, with "spinsters" or "bachelor uncles" being the anomaly.

Today the choice to undertake a sacramental marriage must be more deliberate. For while fewer Catholics are being married or staying married in the Church, those that do are more likely to give serious thought to what God desires from this form of vowed life.[15]

In the Rite of Marriage, husbands and wives vow to "accept children lovingly from God and bring them up according to the law of Christ and his Church" and to be faithful to each other "for better, for worse, for richer, for poorer, in sickness and in health, until death do us part." The language of these vows is sacred, enjoining couples to consider family life as ordained by God and part of his unfolding plan for the welfare of all people.

Historically, the vocation to family was understood to flow out of the vocation to married life. For many, that connection is still a lived reality, but for others, as we've noted, the reality is different. In all cases, though, the vocation to family means a readiness to understand that one's happiness is intimately tied up in the happiness of others in the family.

Work, no matter which model one embraces, cannot be an exclusive good in itself. It must also be an instrumental good, in the sense that it provides a means by which one provides for the family. Even in cases when one does work for the enjoyment of it—let's imagine a case of someone who is wealthy and need not work—the call to work still fulfills emotional, creative, or social needs that spill over into one's family life. Family life is an other-centered vocation, constantly changing because children are always growing. And their growth means that even from one year to the next, the texture of life undergoes great change.

In our experience, raising children is an invitation to an often profoundly meditative way of being-in-time. Whereas the workday ticks by with predictable regularity, punctuated by meetings, tasks, and to-do lists, family life exists in a different kind of time. Especially when our kids were younger, it felt as if we had to take off the workaday world's approach to time as if it were an overcoat and enter a new world with them. Fredrick Buechner puts it beautifully:

> For a child, time in the sense of something to measure and keep track of, time as the great circus parade of past, present, and future, cause and effect, has scarcely started yet and means little because for a child all time is by and large *now* time and apparently endless. What child, while summer is happening, bothers to think much that summer will end? What child, when snow is on the ground, stops to remember that not long ago the ground was snowless? It is by its content rather than its duration that a child knows time, by its quality rather than its quantity—happy times and sad times.[16]

Buechner puts his finger on one of the great gifts of the family vocation: God's invitation to dwell within *his* time in a way reminiscent of our own childhoods. It is very easy—and always tempting—to treat time as a commodity when we are busy. Even now, as we write this, we have one eye on the clock for the next item on the day's to-do list. In a busy life, scheduling happens because of the desire to accomplish many things—many good things!—especially when they have to do with cultivating important relationships. (In the coming hours, for example, we are looking forward to spending some one-on-one time with our children.)

Yet even in the midst of these demands, it is possible to discern God's voice saying, in effect, the words of Jesus to the disciples when they found themselves getting too busy: "Come away by yourselves to a deserted place and rest a while." The Evangelist Mark describes the scene: "People were coming and going in great numbers, and they had no opportunity even to eat" (6:31). Jesus' invitation to rest comes after he has sent the disciples off to preach in various villages and towns in the vicinity: he has, in a word, commissioned them. As parents, we too have been commissioned: that is, "co-missioned," sent with God's Holy Spirit to do the works of mercy in our families. Yet even in the midst of this vocation, Jesus calls to us to rest a while: to dwell in that sacred time away from the constantly ticking clock of our adult lives.

Called to Serve

The vocation to family life, like any vocation in the Church, is a particular kind of invitation to work in a way that builds God's kingdom. Unlike the pessimistic view of work as a consequence of sin—the remnant of God's curse upon Adam and Eve[17]—the work that builds a family's life is almost by definition saturated with meaningfulness. The Lord calls us to participate in the very work of creation itself, perhaps by helping fashion a child within a mother's womb or by helping construct the personhood of the child through rearing. That work is often hard, calling us to go places we might not choose to go, were it not for the needs of our children.

> Building a family benefits parents and children alike, but it also has the potential to benefit others.

Every parent we know has had to face trials, whether the illness of a child, or issues at school, or social problems, or any number of others. Parents lose sleep, make and change plans, negotiate and argue, spend hours on homework, take days off from work to be with their children, plan vacations around school schedules, and so much more. Family work can often be demanding, and sometimes it pushes us to despair.

On the other hand, this work can be profoundly joyful: celebrating our children's successes, enjoying holidays or other celebrations as fruits of much preparation and planning, taking time together to play games or engage in leisure activities, and reflecting on warm memories and shared experiences. The texture of family life over the years varies, including times of sun and rain, consolation and desolation. It is, in a word, life itself, life that the Lord invites us to live to the full (see John 10:10).[18]

Those who enter fully into the vocation to family life will understand how the various relationships within the family constitute the focal points of their ministry. For while work outside the home may be necessary to the family's survival, still it is secondary to the fundamental call to serve the family. According to the Church, the Christian family is "a sign and image of the communion of the Father and the Son in the Holy Spirit" and is called the *"domestic church."*[19]

If we could imagine the way that God sees human work, we would see the call to family life as a fundamental participation in the building of his kingdom, far exceeding many other forms of work that are valued and rewarded in ways disproportionate to their contributions to the good of human society. Is there anything more noble, more beautiful, or more consequential to the social good than the work that flows from a mother's love? Is there anything stronger, more meaningful, more sublime than the way a father gives of himself to his family?

The family vocation is also one that redounds to the benefit of society. As the "original cell of social life" and "an initiation into life in society,"[20] it represents the way that human beings practice what it means to live in community. As parents, we have the opportunity to shape the future by being attentive to our vocation. Building a family benefits parents and children alike, but it also has the potential to benefit others. Practicing a spirituality that nourishes the family means allowing God's grace to ripple outward to neighbors, teammates, coaches and teachers, other parents, and many others. Perhaps you have had experiences of hearing from other adults how your children have impressed them, perhaps through their manners or way of interacting? These are small clues to the contagion of grace, extending from face to face because of the willingness to embrace one's vocation to parenting.

In light of this vocational call, the question of balance between work and family takes on new meaning. For when we allow ourselves to reflect on how God calls us to be ministers of the gospel of family life, we can see our choices about work (and play and everything else) as contributing to the end to which God has called us. To say it a little differently, if we keep in mind that our families are the center of the lives for which God has created us, then all the time we are given in this life has the potential of being a time for the unfolding of God's will. Reclaiming family time becomes a matter of remembering what is most important, keeping priorities, and discerning the way forward. It is not simply about avoiding work, nor is it fundamentally a matter of trying to expand leisure time. Instead, it involves considering which choices benefit the dynamics of family life.

Sometimes, to be sure, reclaiming family time will mean making a priority of leisure time—more on this in a later chapter. But other times, it may involve carving out individual time as a couple, or one-on-one time with a child needing attention, or an opportunity to visit with a teacher or coach. It may involve devoting enough time to work outside the home that opens up opportunities for flexibility at a later stage of family life. We are not suggesting in this book an easy recipe for reclaiming family time. Rather, we are pointing to how Christian spirituality must always be a spirituality of discernment, and how that discernment process unfolds in a particular way within the context of a family.

Reclaiming family time is not only about setting aside a few chunks of time during the week when the family gets together.

Something more fundamental is at stake: the work of reclaiming all time, the Lord's time, as time within which the family undertakes its role as agents of the kingdom.

Questions for Discernment

1. Which of the six approaches to work best describes you? Your spouse? (Work, Career, Passion, Kinship, Craftsmanship, Service)

2. Where are you in your family life cycle? Are you still discerning a career path and how your family life will fit into that path? Or are you established in your career and looking for ways to find more time with your family?

3. What are the time demands of your work? Do you have any opportunity for flexibility?

4. Are there ways you might strategically plan your work in the coming years so that you might have more family time? What are your concerns about the impact on your career?

CHAPTER TWO

Will We Serve the Lord?

*As for me and my household,
we will serve the* LORD.
—Joshua 24:15

t is not without some irony that we were asked to write this book right before we embarked upon one of the busiest and most stressful periods of our lives. We had some grand illusions about conducting some kind of family experiment: "Let's totally get rid of cell phones and TV!" "Maybe we can resolve to do all the corporal and spiritual works of mercy as a family this year!" "Let's reboot family prayer or devote time each night to some kind of game or leisure activity!" But all these grand ideas dissolved into the simple realities of daily life, a life in which there was the potential of a job change and even a move to another state.

So while the idea of a family experiment started out as attractive, what quickly became apparent to us is that any attempt at reclaiming family life had to be rooted in a realistic understanding of the ordinary challenges that shaped our life choices. Sure, a yearlong safari would refocus us as a family; a year living on a desert island might make us less prone to distraction. But these experiences—aside from being far removed from most families' experiences—are not the lives we are actually living. We work for a living and can't immerse ourselves in lives of leisure.

> Reclaiming family life is about listening to the voice of God with what St. Benedict calls "the ear of the heart."

Thinking about the ordinary pressures of our lives made us stop and think about how free we were to reclaim our family life from busyness. We parents have to work in order to pay the bills. The kids have school, time with friends, and activities that they enjoy. In theory, it would be possible to strip down our lives to basic necessities so that (for example) we didn't need as much money and we didn't need to be driving around all the time depositing our kids at a hundred different locations over the course of a week. But would that "scorched earth" approach really help us as a family, or would it only cause resentment? We needed to think more carefully about the balance we struck between work and kids' activities, especially.

For us, reclaiming family life is about listening to the voice of God with what St. Benedict calls "the ear of the heart." Discernment is sifting our experiences, desires, fears, hopes, needs, and relationships to find wisdom.[21] Being asked to write this book gave us the opportunity to discern the complex dynamics that shape family life:

- Our approach to our work
- The demands of school
- The way we use free time as a family
- The way we use money
- The activities our children are engaged in
- The way we use the physical space in our home
- The time our kids spend with friends
- Our activities both together and as individuals
- Our use of technology
- The way we relate to one another
- What we worship and how we pray
- How we balance time together and time alone

There are many more factors that we've discovered too. But what quickly became clear to us as we began to study the topic—about which there is no small amount of research in recent years—is that we needed to establish our frame of reference. By this, we mean something like the place where you stand to look at something: your perspective. Is understanding overscheduling about becoming more efficient? Maximizing a competitive advantage? Having more leisure? Cultivating the best relationships? There seemed to be many ways to look at the question.

So in clarifying where we stood, we considered what we hold to be the most fundamental, bedrock truths by which we live our lives. The words of Joshua to the Israelites came to mind. Joshua is reminding them of what the Lord has done for them by leading them out of Egypt to the Promised Land,

and he challenges them to consider what they will make priorities in their lives.

> Now, therefore, fear the LORD and serve him completely and sincerely. Cast out the gods your ancestors served beyond the River and in Egypt, and serve the LORD. If it is displeasing to you to serve the LORD, choose today whom you will serve, the gods your ancestors served beyond the River or the gods of the Amorites in whose country you are dwelling. As for me and my household, we will serve the LORD. (Joshua 24:14-15)

Joshua challenges his kinspeople to understand what should be most important in their lives—the center around which all of their life choices are to revolve. Will they keep the covenant that the Lord established with their father Abraham? Will they obey the laws given to them through Moses? Or will they slowly drift toward worship of other gods?

Today gods are all around us: wealth, prestige, attractiveness, power, popularity, pleasure, success, intelligence, fashion, convenience, and many others. These are the gods of those in whose country we are dwelling, and they demand worship, in the form of dedicating our energy and our time toward their service. We run around frantically trying to serve them, teaching our children to serve them; we feel rushed, harried, sleep deprived, and anxious. Joshua's exhortation challenges us as it challenged the ancient Israelites: as for us and our household, will we serve the Lord?

For us, that question is not just about what we do on Sunday morning. It's about what sort of work we do and what we think money should be used for. It's about what we want to teach our children about people, about life's meaning, about love and suffering. It's about whether in the hard times—loss of jobs, death of loved ones, stresses in relationships, and so on—we choose the way of Jesus or some other way. It's about priorities like compassion, forgiveness, mercy, generosity, largeness of heart, humility, and sacrifice, even when the benefits of those priorities are not always obvious. It's about living with the faith we learn from the Bible and practice (sometimes well, sometimes badly) in our relationships with others.

> Through prayer we come to understand what is most important in life so that we don't get trapped in the small stuff.

This book became for us an opportunity to think and talk about what we *hope* our priorities are, but also, practically, about what they *actually look like* in everyday life. And what we've discovered is that there can be a gap between our ideals and our reality. Thinking about overscheduling has reminded us that our deepest desire is to serve the Lord and to teach our children to do the same.

Hints from Scripture

In the midst of thinking about the sorts of questions we ought to be asking, we came to Mass one day when the readings were particularly relevant. Have you ever had that kind of experience, as though the Lord had opened your ears to hear something? (We find that one of the great benefits of regular prayer is that kind of attentiveness—"Let those with ears hear," writes Matthew, cf. 11:15.) The first reading was from the book of Wisdom, that collection of meditations and reflections on life that an Egyptian Jew wrote, in imitation of King Solomon, only several decades before the coming of Christ. He writes,

> Who knows God's counsel,
>   or who can conceive what the Lord intends?
> For the deliberations of mortals are timid,
>   and uncertain our plans.
> For the corruptible body burdens the soul
>   and the earthly tent weighs down the mind with its
>   many concerns.
> Scarcely can we guess the things on earth,
>   and only with difficulty grasp what is at hand;
>   but things in heaven, who can search them out?
>   (Wisdom 9:13-16)

It was that line "the earthly tent weighs down the mind with its many concerns" that really caught our attention. For as parents, it's not hard to imagine the many ways in which our minds and hearts are constantly scattered by activity. A conversation is interrupted by a child needing something immediately. We enter a time of prayer first thing in the morning, only to have people wake up and start making noise. We plan an evening's dinner and come home to learn that different people have made different plans, and so an effort at cooking will largely go to waste. While we are not like the ancient heretics who denied the importance of the body to give heed only to the soul, still we find that sometimes it would be nice to have some uninterrupted time for contemplation.

> The point is to remind ourselves and our children that our faith is the rudder that steers our family through life.

The responsorial psalm that day was equally thought provoking and allowed us a moment to turn our prayer in the direction of the ways we live our lives before the eternity of the Lord. It was from Psalm 90:

You turn humanity back into dust,
    saying, "Return, you children of Adam!"
A thousand years in your eyes
    are merely a day gone by,

Before a watch passes in the night,
    you wash them away;
They sleep,
    and in the morning they sprout again like an herb.
In the morning it blooms only to pass away;
    in the evening it is wilted and withered. . . .

Teach us to count our days aright,
    that we may gain wisdom of heart.

Relent, O LORD! How long?
    Have pity on your servants!
Fill us at daybreak with your mercy,
    that all our days we may sing for joy. . . .
May the favor of the Lord our God be ours.
    Prosper the work of our hands!
    Prosper the work of our hands! (Psalm 90:3-6, 12-14, 17)

How easy it can be for us to get caught up in the needs of the moment! Sometimes we'll talk about "being shot out of a cannon," as, for example, when summer ends and the work and school schedules begin in full force. Suddenly there is activity in every direction: early morning wake-ups; getting ready for the day; driving kids to their schools; hurrying on to work; facing an avalanche of new tasks; scheduling and rescheduling appointments, meetings, practices, get-togethers, events, holidays, and so on—only to have someone reschedule something that requires a reschedule of everything else.

The psalmist reminds us of the simple truth that our lives unfold against the backdrop of eternity. What is a life against such a measure? A thousand years are as a single day; an entire life is but a grain of sand. Only the Lord can "teach us to count our days aright, that we may gain wisdom of heart." The psalm can be read as a reminder to pray each morning that the Lord will keep us mindful of this truth: "Fill us at daybreak with your mercy, that all our days we may sing for joy." For only if we know why we live at all can we make life choices that are not filled with the vanity of which the author of Ecclesiastes writes—see the epigraph at the top of this chapter—but rather filled with a desire that "the favor of the Lord our God be ours."

The Gospel reading that day came from Luke's Gospel, asking those who would follow the Lord what their priorities really were:

> Which of you wishing to construct a tower does not first sit down and calculate the cost to see if there is enough for its completion? Otherwise, after laying the foundation and finding himself unable to finish the work the onlookers should laugh at him and say, "This one began to build but did not have the resources to finish." (Luke 14:28-30)

It is a difficult reading about discipleship: Jesus challenges his listeners to ask where their hearts are and what is really most important to them. He states that anyone who is not willing to put service of the Lord ahead of love of father and mother, wife and children, brothers and sisters, and even one's own life "cannot be my disciple" (Luke 14:26). Why such strong words?

The image that comes to mind will be familiar to anyone who has flown in an airplane. The flight attendant demonstrates the safety features of the plane, indicating that should there be a drop in cabin air pressure, oxygen masks will drop from the ceiling. The attendant's counsel is that you should put on your own mask first before helping a child or someone else who needs it. The priority, in other words, is to do what insures your own life and then to do what is helpful to others.

We read Jesus' counsel in a similar way: he says, do what gives life first—learn from the Lord first in all things. To learn from the Lord, to be his disciple, means meditating on his word day and night. The psalmist puts it beautifully:

> Blessed is the man who does not walk
> in the counsel of the wicked,
> Nor stand in the way of sinners,
> nor sit in company with scoffers.
> Rather, the law of the LORD is his joy;
> and on his law he meditates day and night.
> He is like a tree
> planted near streams of water,
> that yields its fruit in season;
> Its leaves never wither;
> whatever he does prospers. (Psalm 1:1-3)

The point, it seems to us, is not about how prayer gets in the way of having a life. Quite the opposite: through prayer we come to understand what is most important in life so that we don't get trapped in the small stuff.

Stephen Covey, the leadership guru, used an image that we find helpful. Imagine an empty jar into which a person tries to fit large rocks, small rocks, sand, and water. If she begins with the water or the sand, there will be no room for all the large and small rocks. But if she starts with the big rocks, then adds the small rocks, then the sand and lastly the water, it can all fit into the jar. Similarly, if one begins with the big rocks in life—the most important priorities—and later attends to the lesser priorities and only later the daily things calling for our attention, life will not become overcrowded. Big rocks first!

Family time itself is wholly good, sufficient unto itself, a glimpse of the kingdom.

Our challenge is to call to mind what is most important on a daily basis: to root ourselves in prayer. Only when we see our lives with this highest priority in mind do we really see what is worth doing and what is worth letting go. Don't get us wrong—we don't always live up to this priority—but when we look at the course of our lives, we can see the ways that God has been faithful when we have been willing to listen to him. If being rooted in prayer is, to use Covey's term, a "big rock," then the smaller rocks, pebbles, and water are a little easier to fit in. Not that the goal in life is to have a completely full jar—instead the goal is first to be who God has created us to be in relationship to others and to see all our other priorities in the light of that vocation.

A Discernment Exercise: Big Rocks

Consider the following reflective exercise. If you are a single parent, find a few minutes, perhaps at the end of the day or at a time when you won't be hounded for attention. If you are married, have a conversation with your spouse. The point of this exercise is to begin to identify the different rocks, pebbles, sand, and water in your life, in order that you might come to some clarity about the ways you use time as a family. Consider the questions that are most relevant, rather than spending time on all of them. It may be best to spread these out over several days or even weeks.

1. What are the concrete ways you root your family life in prayer? How do you practice your faith and share it with your children?

2. What are the ways you have taught your children the relationship between faith and service to others?

3. How do you insure that your children learn and grow in their faith? What books or websites do they use?

4. Who are the people in your family's life that support and nourish your shared faith?

5. How do you celebrate significant milestones in your family's faith life (baptisms, first reconciliations, first Communions, confirmations, weddings)?

6. How do you make worship a priority in your family's life? Is going to Mass a focal point of your week?

7. How do you nourish your own faith? Do you make time for prayer?

Practices

The questions above are focused on making prayer a focal point of both personal and family life. In practice, that need not take up as much time as other important pursuits like work or school, but we are convinced that in order for it to be central in a family's life, there must be concrete ways each member of the family experiences it. So first, a broad question, paraphrasing C. S. Lewis: if your family was accused of being Christian, what evidence would people find? How does your family carry on a living conversation with God?

Over our years of parenting, we have found that there is almost never a consistent answer to that question, save one: we go to Mass. For us, the Mass is the central act of Christian worship around which the rest of our life revolves. At every stage of our children's lives—from noisy infancy, to rambunctious toddlerhood, to antsy youth, to bored teenagehood—our consistent message is that Sundays (and some Saturday vigils) are built around planning for Mass. Whether we are at home or away, we find a way to pray together. As our kids have gotten older, it has become increasingly difficult to maintain this practice. Sports schedules, work schedules, and events with friends slowly eat away opportunities to worship together. More frequently of late, we've had to split up our Mass going: some go early, others late.

Mass is important to us for many reasons. On a basic level, it remains the only activity that all of us share outside of family dinner. (And it is, of course, another kind of family meal.) Our kids' growing autonomy means that there are very few things that we can all do without grimaces all around. But that's not the only reason, or even the best reason. For us adults—who have studied a little history and theology—the Mass is a rich place of encounter with Christ through the Eucharist, the words of Scripture, and the people with whom we share worship. We hope that over time, and as they grow into deeper understanding, our kids will begin to connect the words they hear from the ambo with the sacramental practice they see unfolding at the altar.

We have always loved how tactile and experiential the Mass is: there are images and sounds all around the church; there are people attending to the words and actions of the liturgical ministers and the priest; there is the steady stream of souls seeking nourishment as they process toward Communion. We often wonder how this rich milieu strikes our kids' imagination at their different ages, and we rejoice when we see some evidence—however small—that their lives bear the imprint of what we celebrate together at church.

But as rich as the Mass is for us, we realize that much of that richness is lost on kids, who can be fidgety at any age. So over the years, we have thought about the ways in which we might connect that experience of worship with other forms of prayer at home. Our hope is that deepening our kids' (and our own) toolbox of prayer can help us be mindful of the Lord's presence with us, even on a daily basis.

Some of our practices are fairly traditional, while others are homegrown. We've used the customary prayers before meals ("Bless us, O Lord, and these, thy gifts . . . ") and before bed ("Now I lay me down to sleep . . . "). We've issued blessings to our kids with the laying on of hands, as on the first day of school or before an important event or performance. We've adapted the Ignatian Examen prayer in age-appropriate ways.[22] We've used various forms of prayer during the seasons of Advent and Lent. We've celebrated liturgies in schools and on vacations. We pray often for people in our lives who are in situations of need: illness, death of loved ones, financial or job stress. And there are many others.

For us, the point is to remind ourselves and our children that our faith is the rudder that steers our family through life. It is a source of meaning and of comfort in hard times; it is a source of challenge to be mindful of others. For us, the basic logic is that of Aristotle, who observed that we become what we do. We don't want to just think about faith—we want to enact it.

There is an ancient image of a life well lived: it is like a jar of honey, full of sweetness. In contrast, a life lived badly is like a jar of vinegar. For the ancients, the sweetness of honey was a reflection of the industriousness of the bees who made it. Not a bad image—particularly if we remember that bees are not simply creatures who work nonstop. They stop and (almost literally) smell the roses! But fundamentally, bees are active creatures: they exist for a purpose and work together to achieve it.

In the midst of our busy lives, it's easy to get lost in the small stuff. Centering ourselves on prayer through concrete practices is a reminder that our lives, both as individuals and as a family, have meaning and purpose and that our choices and actions ought to serve that end. One fruit of prayer is the recognition that we are, in the words of St. Ignatius of Loyola, "created to praise, reverence, and serve God our Lord" above all else, and that any element of daily life might thus be oriented toward that end. Nothing else is really an end in itself: not work, not making the house clean, not any athletic event, not even leisure time.

So our approach to reclaiming family time is not only about carving out unused spaces of time and populating them with various kinds of leisure. Instead it's about bringing our desire to "serve God our Lord" into all things: cleaning the kitchen with each other, working on kids' homework, shuttling to and from games and practices, watching a movie.

For us, the challenge is to have the right attitude so that ordinary practices of family life become opportunities to grow in the purpose for which God has created us—that is, to bring a contemplative attitude into everyday life.

Contemplation

The Carmelite William McNamara has described contemplation as "a long loving look at the real."[23] Commenting on this description, the theologian Walter Burghardt observed that what often gets in the way of contemplation is a well-trained attitude to look for utility in all things. Such an attitude, he suggests, is deeply engrained into our Western minds because of a certain default philosophy about life. Everything must be useful; our time must be dedicated to some Important Goal, whether for ourselves or our children. Our collective hours at work have increased; our demands for our children have similarly increased. It's not enough that they do homework during the school year; they must also take classes over the summer and go to math camp. In our part of the country, there is a dizzying array of structured summer options but almost no free play among neighborhood kids. And let's not even start talking about preparing for college!

Contemplation is the opposite of usefulness. According to McNamara, contemplation is "a pure intuition of being, born of love. It is experiential awareness of reality and a way of entering into immediate communion with reality." It is the willingness to hit pause and to see others the way God does.

For parents, it means suspending the tendency to subject our children to ever more planning and scheduling and being willing to see them in the simple reality of being lovable, loved by God, entrusted to our care for a few years.

Contemplation is itself a practice, especially since it represents a critical posture toward the utilitarian ethic that shapes so much of our attitudes toward life. Don't get us wrong: we do not pretend to suggest that it's possible to check out of the need to do useful things, like work for a living and pay bills. Instead, we are suggesting that in the midst of doing the things necessary to run a household, God invites us into a relationship characterized by contemplation rather than utility. God invites us to see the world and each other not through the lens of utility but rather through the lens of contemplation.

What does this mean? For us, as we have said, it means first the regular practice of prayer and worship, through which we develop the habit of seeing the world as Jesus did. "The law of the LORD is his joy; / and on his law he meditates day and night," wrote the psalmist (1:2).

Second, it means practicing acts of self-giving and helping our children learn such practices. Making dinner for a sick neighbor, serving at a shelter for homeless people in our region, distributing clothing to the poor in the city—these and other acts are ways that we remind ourselves of the love that the Lord has for all his beloved children, whether or not they have glamorous jobs or good education. These and the many other ways that we seek to make real what we profess at Mass help us to be mindful that the Lord's ways are not our ways and that our ways can often be caught up in desires for immediate benefits that do not serve the kingdom.

The fruit of contemplation is, among other things, an encounter with beauty. For the person who sees people through contemplative eyes cannot miss the ways that their actions often shine forth God's grace—even when they themselves might miss it. We have on many occasions been struck by what we see in our daily lives: interruptions of the usual drive to accomplish what is immediately necessary (homework, chores, shopping, and so on) by actions that can freeze time for a moment because of their delightfulness. A sister who teaches a brother chords on a ukulele, a brother who goes out of his way to fill his sister's water bottle, a sister who unexpectedly takes time to play basketball with a brother, a brother who offers a sister part of his burrito.

These are small actions, easy to overlook in the course of a too busy day; but through eyes trained in contemplation, they are windows to the workings of divine grace. And we wouldn't want to miss them for the world.

Reclaiming Family Time

In a fast-paced life, one great challenge to practicing a contemplative life is simple weariness—that cumulative effect of constantly being on the run to keep up with the demands of daily life. Every so often, we need to recharge our spiritual batteries. And as a family like many others—ordered to a large extent around the school calendar—that usually happens during the summer.

Last summer, though, was something of a blur. Usually we like to start thinking about the summer early in the year, when the weather in New England is cold and thoughts of lounging at the beach are far away. The previous year, we had been able to plan an extended getaway, visiting with family in Georgia and then taking a trip to Florida. That experience had been a high-water mark for us, allowing us a chance to relax, rejuvenate, and enjoy some time together at a point when our kids were growing in their independence. This year, though, several factors were working against us: we were discerning the possibility of a move, one of our kids was old enough to work and had a summer work schedule that made it hard to plan a vacation, money was tight. Before we knew it, school had ended and we had no specific plans.

We started off on a good foot, heading off camping with some friends. We caught a glorious weekend in the White Mountains of New Hampshire and enjoyed hiking and sightseeing—though we discovered in the process that two of our three kids had become adamant in their dislike of camping. So we had to cross that off the list of possible ways to reclaim some family time in the future. After that first weekend, we fell into a pleasant though somewhat scattered typical summer pattern. Our teen and preteen kids are more adept at making their own plans, so we found that most days were a mix of trips with one child to the pond for swimming, another child heading off to work, and a third making plans to get together with friends. There were some periods at home, maybe watching a movie together, but for the most part, we found that our family members were heading in different directions. The pace was good and we enjoyed the free time, but on the whole, this otherwise relaxing time of year was taking us away from each other. And with both of us parents needing still to be mindful of work commitments, we felt the summer slowly slipping away.

We had a nagging sense that some kind of interruption of our schedule was necessary. Our time was getting chopped up in various activities—many of them fun in themselves, but overall lacking a sense of purpose. (Later in this book, we'll talk about different approaches to time and dwell at length on how a robust understanding of leisure is important for us as individuals and families.) We intuited that it was important to find some dedicated time for us *as a family* in spite of the difficulties we had experienced in planning our summer. We brought this desire into prayer and hoped that there might be some way to carve out that time.

What happened was a confluence of circumstances, which in retrospect we attribute to God's grace. First, our daughter who was working all summer had a new job prospect open up that interrupted the schedule of two other jobs she was working, and suddenly there was a long weekend that was free. Second, we received an invitation to spend time at a place in nearby Vermont—a drive long enough to get away but short enough not to cost an arm and a leg. We jumped at the opportunity, clearing our own schedules enough to take four nights in the mountains at a lovely town house.

One of the graces of a real vacation is that it immediately suspends the usual value of time. More on this later—but the impression it left on us all was being able to just stop and be in the moment, with each other. Neither of us has any illusions about the way kids will understand this point—they still want something to do, now—but what we observed was that even they recognized the benefit of not having to be at someone else's beck and call. The experience as a whole was a practice in contemplation: we slowed down, enjoyed meals together, went and did fun activities—and none of them had any purpose beyond recreation. On the whole, the experience of those four days and nights was that family time itself is wholly good, sufficient unto itself, a glimpse of the kingdom.

It is very telling that, according to Burghardt, practicing contemplation requires first an experience of the desert. The desert, of course, is the place where, in both the Bible and the early Church, one goes to encounter the Lord: Moses and the burning bush; Elijah and the cave; Jesus withdrawing to be with his Father; Anthony, Mary of Egypt, and the other desert fathers and mothers. The desert is the experience of withdrawal from the urgencies of life, those pressing needs that constantly extract from us energy and attention. In the desert we confront what is most basic, most fundamental in life, and we see our usual activities in a new perspective. For us, even a four-day vacation—if that is all we can afford—is a kind of desert.

Second, Burghardt suggests that festivity and play are integral to the contemplative attitude. Both of these kinds of experiences are the opposite of utility: they draw us into the gift of the moment. Thanksgiving dinners, religious holidays, family birthdays, and other celebrations remind us to enjoy the time we have and call to mind how quickly life passes from one year to the next. We see the same decorations, eat the same foods, and enjoy the same celebrations, each year taking note of how our children—and we ourselves—have changed.

Similarly, playtime, whether wiffle ball in the yard or a game of Monopoly during a rainstorm, is an experience of the now. Play can be an experience of sufficiency, eliciting the kind of response that Peter expressed upon seeing Jesus transfigured: it is good to be here. It is doubtful that when we are very old, we will recall fondly the days we spent at work or paying taxes. But we will assuredly remember experiences of play with our children and, God willing, our grandchildren.

Questions for Discernment

1. How would you describe your fundamental attitude toward time?
   a. Is it a precious commodity that you spend like a miser?
   b. Is it a gift that you love to give to others?
   c. Is it comprised of a series of surprises?
   d. Is it something you are in control of?
   e. Is it something you dread?
   f. Or something else?

2. If you were brought to a court of law and your life were under examination, what evidence would the prosecution bring against you to demonstrate what you find most important in life?

3. How do you prioritize your faith? What are the concrete ways your faith is obvious to your children?

4. Psalm 90 describes our lives unfolding against the backdrop of eternity. How might you remind yourself of this truth on a daily basis? How can you remind yourself of the "big rocks" in your life?

5. For Catholics, the preeminent practice of faith is the Eucharist—a gift to share with your family. Other devotions also can develop in us the habit of receiving the Lord's gift of time. What devotions does your family practice, or what devotions could be easily added to your daily life?

6. Contemplation is the practice of coming to see the beauty in everyday life. It is the opposite of usefulness. In what ways can you interrupt the flow of "useful" time in order to experience life more contemplatively?

CHAPTER THREE

Leisure

*[N]ature herself, as has been often said, requires that
we should be able, not only to work well, but to use
leisure well; for, as I must repeat once again, the first
principle of all action is leisure.*
—Aristotle, *Politics* 8.3

*He said to them, "Come away by yourselves
to a deserted place and rest a while."*
—Mark 6:31

One of the graces of parenting is the regular practice of
seeing the world through the eyes of children. Before
we started writing this chapter, we spent some time
picnicking at a nearby lake, watching the sunset. A family festival had just concluded, so we walked onto the beach as adults
were cleaning up and kids were darting to and fro in the sand.
It was delightful watching the children, who were as carefree
as the birds as their parents collected belongings and moved
coolers and blankets out to their cars in the parking lot.

The image of Mary and Martha came to mind—the story
of the two sisters who are hosting Jesus. Martha is busy with
the details of being a good hostess, while Mary simply sits at

Jesus' feet, enjoying his presence (see Luke 10:38-42). Jesus answers Martha's complaint about her unhelpful sister by saying that Mary has chosen the better part. The kids at the beach, too, chose the better part. It was a beautiful evening, the sunset was beautiful, and they were free to run around and play with their friends. Life was beautiful.

The scene elicited some nostalgia as we reflected on our teens' growing-up years. Gone are the days of frolicking unselfconsciously on the beach with friends. Now, our children's leisure time is comprised of very teen-like, self-conscious nights out on the town. And while we miss those days of play, we nevertheless appreciate the opportunity to thank God that we took time at that stage in our kids' lives to make a priority of leisure time together. In retrospect, we realize that carving out times like those took effort and sacrifice, especially in regard to our work lives.

Leisure time changes dramatically over the course of a family's life. We find ourselves marking the passage of time when we see opportunities for leisure activities that we once enjoyed but have grown out of. But what remains constant is the sense that it is still important to find ways that all of us can spend leisure time together. For that shared leisure time is a foretaste of heaven. How, we often wonder, might we order our lives in ways that allow for more of it?

One immediately obvious response to that question is to point out that not all people have the luxury of having time away from work, especially the working poor. We've had periods in our lives when leisure was not even something we could think about wanting more of because we were struggling to make ends meet. So on one level, even the question about how to recover some leisure time is itself a luxury that not all people can afford.

Yet there is a deeper level to this question that is the subject of this chapter. Our culture has lost its understanding of what makes leisure possible and so has compromised the ability of many individuals and families to find it. Our reflection on leisure, therefore, is far from being a how-to guide for people who have lots of money to spend on their vacations. Instead it is a meditation on a classical understanding of leisure, which, we are convinced, is rooted in a much more substantial grasp of what all our activity ought to be oriented toward.

Leisure is not only for the rich—it is for everyone who seeks to live wisely.

In this classical understanding, we'll illustrate, leisure is *what we work for* and involves the activities that help us recover something fundamental about ourselves. Leisure, in this understanding, is not only for the rich—it is for everyone who seeks to live wisely.

What Is Leisure?

In his *Divine Comedy*, Dante offers an image that is the opposite of leisure. It is an image of those souls in purgatory who have lived selfishly proud lives and who, as a consequence of always thinking about themselves, must carry around crushingly heavy boulders—the consequence of what they have worked to build for themselves over the course of their lives. For Dante there is a temptation to treat work as an extension of selfish pride— pointless in itself save for the way that it can inflate a person's ego. In contrast, he offers images of people who have learned the proper relationship between themselves and God and who, as a consequence, are not tempted to make an idol of their work. There is Mary, the mother of Jesus, who describes herself as "the handmaid of the Lord," and King David, who dances even in the presence of servants out of an exuberant joy at the presence of the Lord.[24] These figures, Dante suggests, are capable of joy because they know themselves to be at the service of God.

If we follow Dante's logic, the difference between the selfishly proud and the virtuously humble is right relationship to God and thus a right attitude toward work that makes leisure possible. Leisure, in the classical view, emerges as the fruit of a certain modesty and orientation toward God's truth. St. Augustine describes it this way: "The attraction of leisure ought not to be empty-headed inactivity, but in the quest or discovery of truth, both for [one's] own progress and for the purpose of sharing ungrudgingly with others."[25] His view reflects that of Aristotle centuries earlier who observed that the reason people work is so that they might have leisure. If the *Jeopardy!* answer is "leisure," the question, Aristotle suggests, is "beyond the basic necessities of life, why do we work at all?"

But there's a deeper level to leisure that Aristotle seeks to unpack in his meditations on the good life. He notes that the usual pattern of activity involves work and recreation or entertainment—a pattern that we certainly see in our daily lives. We go to work or school, do what needs to be done, then come home and do various chores like make dinner and clean the house. Maybe there's time to watch a TV show or listen to some music, but soon everyone's tired and goes to bed. It's a pretty common cycle. What Aristotle notices, though, is that beyond the usual work-entertain-rest pattern is a deeper desire for leisure, which he describes in his *Politics* as the proper object of the best part of us—our intellect.

Recently we were having a talk with one of our children that reflected Aristotle's critique. (And no, we did not specifically mention Aristotle in the conversation.) The conversation went something like this: We observed that our child tends to fill time with playing on an electronic device. We raised the concern that playing on the device was becoming all-consuming, eating up time that might be used on other kinds of activities, and that we wanted to encourage more creative uses of time.

We spent a while talking about different ways of using time, and these different ideas were reflections on what constitutes leisure. We pointed to the difference between watching TV— an almost entirely passive activity—and playing outside with friends. Playing with friends, we noted (in so many words), involves creativity, imagination, and relationship building. It nourishes parts of ourselves and is life-giving in a way that watching TV is not. Similarly, we pointed to activities like making music, drawing, or building things with Legos—all of which draw on skills worth cultivating. We even acknowledged that some video games require creativity and intellect and that various forms of social media can involve learning relationship skills. All these things can be good.

In general, we were trying to invite our child to reflect on the difference between active and passive uses of time and the various ways that entertainment and recreational activities build us up or leave us listless. We hoped that raising these issues might help our child to see the way that leisure is the opportunity to give ourselves what our souls need.

Our souls crave leisure: that is, they crave the nourishment that more simple pleasures can never offer. Seeking pleasure rather than leisure is like seeking candy rather than a nourishing meal: both pleasure and candy offer temporary highs, followed by dispiritedness and weariness. Paradoxically, suggests Aristotle, leisure demands a kind of being-at-work, for it takes effort to engage in activity that nourishes the soul. In contrast to pleasure, which often means a kind of passive reception of stimuli (think of lounging on the couch watching TV or even attending a sporting event), leisure is an active condition: a state of activity that is good for its own sake and that yields happiness as a by-product.[26]

The opposite of the active condition of leisure is mindless inactivity. In early Christianity, there developed a doctrine of the "deadly sins," those practices that flow out of desires that have become focused too much on ourselves and not enough on God. We've already pointed to the way that Dante illustrates one of them—sinful pride, defined as a kind of worship of the self rather than the proper worship of God. Another one of the deadly sins is *acedia*, which is often translated as "sloth" or inactivity. The reason why acedia became regarded as a deadly sin is because it is ultimately resigning oneself to a state of passivity, saying "whatever" to the world as though nothing really mattered. (It may well be the cardinal sin of many teens, but that's a different book.)

Seeking pleasure rather than leisure is like seeking candy rather than a nourishing meal: both pleasure and candy offer temporary highs, followed by dispiritedness and weariness.

In the classical world, good living demanded action, a certain vigilance in seeking to do the good even at great cost to oneself. In Dante's purgatory, which is a place of purification of desire so that one can enter heaven, the penalty for acedia is having to constantly run around, shouting examples of slothful behavior and contrary examples of acting decisively. His example is again Mary, who in her joy at conceiving Jesus in her womb rushes to meet her kinswoman Elizabeth in order to share her joy. That image—of rejoicing at some goodness and seeking to share it with family—is our model for authentic leisure, and it informs our understanding of how to reclaim family time in a way that reflects who God calls us to be.

An Ordered Life

The twentieth-century philosopher Josef Pieper wrote an extended essay on leisure that takes as its point of departure the thesis that culture depends on leisure and that leisure is not possible unless it is related to worship.[27] His insight is as applicable to the family as it is to entire civilizations, and it has shaped the way that we think about the aim of our family time.

For Pieper, worship is absolutely central: what we worship is that toward which we devote all our energies. He is speaking broadly about the practical ways that we structure our time, both as individuals and as families: what do we really live for? Is it money? Security? Outdoing our neighbors? Having the latest technology? In a related vein, the question about worship affects our approach to work and free time. What are we working for? What is our attitude toward free time? Are work and free time creative and positive, or are they varying forms of drudgery?

Everyone must choose what to worship—what to make the central point of one's life—and this is equally true of families. True worship means asking the fundamental question of what is worth living for. Failing to ask that question means handing over our freedom to the pursuit of whatever end the rest of the culture says is worth pursuing. And in much of the world today, that answer is money.

To worship the Lord is to resist making everything a means to an end that we have not chosen for ourselves. Real freedom, in this sense, is detachment from the useful, the efficient, the practical—and even from "common sense," which is little more than agreeing with everyone else even if they are fundamentally misguided. Pieper says it well:

> Thus, the act of worship creates a store of real wealth which cannot be consumed by the workaday world. It sets up an area where calculation is thrown to the winds and goods are deliberately squandered, where usefulness is forgotten and generosity reigns. Such wastefulness is, we repeat, true wealth: the wealth of the feast time. And only in this feast time can leisure unfold and come to fruition.[28]

Real wealth, he suggests, is feast time: the willingness to simply be in the presence of people we cherish to celebrate the life that God has given us. Note that what he is talking about is not simply resting up for work, "recharging the batteries" so we can get back to work. Instead, he is talking about stepping outside the very pattern of work altogether and living in a different mode. Leisure "runs at right angles to work," he suggests; it exists for itself and not for the purpose of making us better worker bees in the economy.[29]

When we look at the long story of our family's life, we see the wisdom in Pieper's ideas. We think about the memories we've captured in photos—Christmases, Thanksgiving dinners, birthdays, adoption days, family trips, and so on. These times are memorable precisely because they represent interruptions from the work that is now part of our lives 24/7, thanks to technology.

Let us be clear: it is not that we dislike our work. Even though there are certainly elements of work that can be draining, for the most part we have been able to do meaningful work that reflects a vocational call. The issue is that even the best work is almost always about building *something other than the family itself*, whereas leisure can be understood as the time during which we build our families. In a rightly ordered life, we are convinced, leisure is not about distraction or entertainment but rather about the joy that comes from seeing our family grow more and more into a good society.

At this writing, we are on the verge of celebrating Christmas. It is the last day of school before the long holiday, and we are all tired from many weeks of work. (Let us acknowledge that while our children attend "school," which comes from the Greek word *scholé*, meaning "leisure," school is indeed their work.) Christmas represents for many the holiday *par excellence*, with everyone devoted to making the experience a rich and memorable one: time with family, recollection of stories, shared food and conversation, the exchange of gifts, and so on.

> Even the best work is almost always about building something other than the family itself, whereas leisure can be understood as the time during which we build our families.

While instructive in many ways, the experience of Christmas is illustrative of a central point we wish to highlight here: namely, that leisure takes a different kind of work. It is work oriented toward the purpose of building life itself, and as such, it is of a kind entirely different from what we earn money for. The hours spent shopping for presents, or preparing meals to be shared, or baking cookies to offer to friends, or visiting relatives—this is a different kind of time and a different form of effort, removed entirely from the daily and monthly calculus of "making a living." It is the work for which we undertake our paid work. It is the work of rejoicing in life itself.

Rejoicing in Life Itself

Dante's image of purgatory is an image of the antidote to the listlessness that comes from failing to do the work that constitutes authentic leisure. Recall the image of Mary running to meet Elizabeth to share the joy of her pregnancy:

> During those days Mary set out and traveled to the hill country in haste to a town of Judah, where she entered the house of Zechariah and greeted Elizabeth. When Elizabeth heard Mary's greeting, the infant leaped in her womb, and Elizabeth, filled with the holy Spirit, cried out in a loud voice and said, "Most blessed are you among women, and blessed is the fruit of your womb. And how does this happen to me, that the mother of my Lord should come to me? For at the moment the sound of your greeting reached my ears, the infant in my womb leaped for joy. Blessed are you who believed that what was spoken to you by the Lord would be fulfilled." (Luke 1:39-45)

Luke describes this scene immediately after the angel of the Lord has come to Mary and announced that she, an as-yet unmarried woman, would become pregnant. We can imagine the stress that would accompany such an announcement, the uncertainty about how this event would upset whatever plans she and her fiancé, Joseph, were making. Luke doesn't give us much detail, but perhaps Mary's escape to visit a cousin was a way of avoiding any gossip among the neighbors.

What makes the scene memorable has little to do with the everyday stresses caused by Mary's new normal. Instead, Luke describes how Mary hastened to be with someone dear to her. He narrates an interchange of a few minutes that constitutes an interruption in the flow of daily life: the simple joy of two women who are giddy with delight at sharing the experience of pregnancy. Their palpable joy spills over even to the child who leaps for joy in Elizabeth's womb. Mothers and sons are there, together, reveling in the goodness of the Lord.

Leisure, for a family, is like that. It is an interruption in the flow of daily life and a celebration of life for its own sake. And the reason that real leisure depends on worship is because only when life is understood as a precious gift of God can people simply stop and appreciate its beauty on its own terms and not as a means to various forms of emotional or intellectual stimulation. Recreation and entertainment may be fun, but they may not really be leisurely in this sense. We discern sometimes a tendency toward frenetic activity, even in our own lives—the sense that every moment must be filled with some kind of activity so no one gets bored.

Now, we are practical people, so we must admit that there can often be a yawning gap between the ideal and reality. We are not trying to suggest that family life depends on frozen moments of heavenly grace shining around beatific smiles on our children's faces as we gaze lovingly on one another in the family room. Quite the contrary: as we have seen, leisure takes work. There is a paradox here, but as we think about the times when we have been able to really enjoy family time, we realize that many of them have taken energy to make happen.

At the risk of falling into abstraction, let us return to an insight of Aristotle, who held that happiness emerges from activity and not as a reward for sitting around doing nothing. His point, we think, is that even the happiness that comes from leisure time is not something magical that just appears and disappears. It must be the object of planning, thoughtfulness, and activity.

For us, a typical example is the day trip. We've become adept at taking advantage of good-weather days, especially during the summer breaks from school. With some flexibility in our work schedules, we've been fortunate to take advantage of beautiful days to head off to a beach or a mountain or some seaside town near where we live. Very often over the years, these day trips have been spontaneous: we take a look at the weather report and spring into action. Someone starts getting the cooler ready, packing lunch and snacks. Someone else will clean out the car (which is usually messy) so everyone has room to sit. Another person may gather up pillows or music to listen to on the drive. When it works well (not every time, but more often as the kids get older), we're able to set off in about an hour and pick a place to go.

We'll seldom have a specific goal in mind. Maybe it will be to sit at the beach and play in the waves. Depending on the weather, we'll take a hike or go "in and out shopping," as one of our daughters once described what you do among the shops in pretty New England towns. Other times, especially in colder weather, we'll just head somewhere beautiful and find a restaurant that has a scenic view where we have lunch. Many of these day trips have required some research—what's the weather? What events or festivals are happening? What's the traffic like? How much will this or that cost? How long will it take to get there? And so on. With six of us (mom, dad, three kids, and Nana), there have been many factors to consider over the years—walking distance, kids' needs for food or drink, stamina, and so on. Sometimes we've failed miserably, but more often we find that these kinds of day trips are refreshing and enjoyable. And they have yielded some wonderful memories.

One Father's Day we took our family on a day trip to the Berkshires in western Massachusetts. We left early on the Sunday morning to drive two hours, first to Mass at the National Shrine of Divine Mercy in Stockbridge, then to a picnic lunch and a hike to see a waterfall in Chester-Blandford State Forest. We drove along the Jacob's Ladder Trail, a scenic byway, soaking in the clean air and sunshine, ending our day with a trip to a great ice cream place and later an outdoor dinner. The day was a chance to relax, recharge, and reconnect, a real gift in the midst of the usual stresses of school and work.

It's become a tradition to give Dad the chance to plan a day trip on Father's Day as a way of regathering our family and enjoying each other's company. Other years, it's been mountain climbing, a baseball game, or a long bike ride. But as the years go on, it gets harder and harder to find activities that our teen and tween kids—as well as their Nana—can enjoy.

> The happiness that comes from leisure time is not something magical that just appears and disappears. It must be the object of planning, thoughtfulness, and activity.

What we've found is that a day sabbath now takes a lot of preparation. We've never had lots of money, so the idea of going to an amusement park or some other expensive plug-and-play activity isn't usually an option. Instead, we've had to scour coupons, look for free or cheap options like parks or beaches, and be creative. We have to take into account tolerance levels (who's willing to walk or bike, for how long), diet (who will eat what, when), distance (how long it takes to drive there), entertainment (how kids will spend time in the car or in the activity), and so on. But more often than not, we have a great time, and so the kids have developed a pretty good sense that our shared leisure can be fun.

When the kids were younger and basically in no position to argue, we could pack up snacks and head in the general direction of somewhere we wanted to be, like the beach or the ski slope. Our rule of thumb was pretty simple: we wanted to interrupt the usual patterns of behavior at home, unplug our kids from their screens, and create opportunities for shared conversation and enjoyment. Over the years, we've developed a stack of memories of places we've visited for day trips, most of which have been very economical.

We've cultivated an adventurous spirit, and so our kids have learned to go along, get along, and be ready for some adventure. We've even gotten in the habit over the last several summers of posting a list on our refrigerator of the places we've gone for our day trips: surfing in Narragansett, sailing in Portsmouth, eating lobster in Gloucester, kayaking in Maine, enjoying great ice cream in New Hampshire, and so on. Our hope is that preserving these summer memories will help our kids develop both a spirit of gratitude and a readiness to make shared leisure a priority in their lives.

We ask ourselves: what makes days like these possible? What are the factors that allow us as a family simply to rejoice in the gift of our life together? One answer, we are convinced, is practicing reverence for the gift of life itself. We sense that fear drives many to prioritize work, such that any time for leisure appears to be a distraction from the demands of work. For us, though, work must be secondary to the gift of life itself. The weekly call to sabbath rest—which we will take up in the next chapter—is fundamentally a reminder that work is not the center of life but rather that which supports what is central. Perhaps you've heard the adage that some people work in order to live but that others live in order to work. For us, leisure is the original state, the state of receiving God's gift of life.

On a practical level, prioritizing leisure time means planning work as well as possible so it doesn't spill over into family time. Do we always do this well? No. But we have some ideals that reflect what we have come to know about ourselves. For example, we try to leave significant chunks of the weekend to leisure. This is often hard because for many years, Sue has been the director of family ministries at our parish, a job that involves working on Sunday mornings for much of the year. But we've become more or less adept at keeping free time on Saturdays and even Sunday afternoons. Similarly, when Tim has lots of grading to do from weekday classes, we try to keep the middle of the day free if he needs time in the morning or evening on those days. Ideally, Saturday and Sunday would be free from work altogether, but often that's just not realistic. So our middle ground is to consider which parts of those days are most likely to offer long stretches of unplanned time.

Another element of prioritizing leisure time means paying attention to seasonal change. Living in New England, it is rather easy to see seasonal change even in an era when we live much of our lives indoors. We think of writers such as Wendell Berry who provoke us to consider the ways in which our modern culture removes us from the natural world, creating a separation between us and nature. We lose touch with ourselves as creatures—part of the whole created order—governed by the same natural forces that affect all living things. We pointed to one effect of this loss of touch earlier when we wrote about our collective lack of sleep, due in part to a loss of understanding of the circadian rhythms that are affected by seasonal change. Attending to things like weather and length of daylight impacts our choices around leisure.

We discovered the importance of this attention several years ago when our daughters' school offered parents the opportunity for their kids to participate in a ski club. It was not something we'd considered before, having grown up in areas far from ski resorts. We wondered about the cost and the time commitment. But several of their friends joined, and so we looked into it and made the decision to let them join as well. Over the course of six weeks, Tim and the girls traveled up to a local ski hill, where the girls got lessons and had a great time with friends.

Reflecting on the experience after the six weeks were over, we marveled at how this investment of money and time yielded unexpected fruit. Not only did the girls have some great experiences with their friends and learn a new skill that would provide opportunities for family fun later on; we also discovered that an otherwise dull indoor time of year was transformed into an opportunity to enjoy the outdoors. We found that we had a higher energy level, likely because of getting exercise and greater exposure to the sunlight. We found that an otherwise cold, dark time of year passed quickly, and before we knew it, spring break was upon us. Plus, Dad and daughters had some fun memories of time together. Mom was able to join in the fun a few times too.

Paying attention to seasonal change for us means thinking primarily in terms of what opportunities we have to reconnect with the natural world that through its beauty invites us to slow down and simply be thankful. Summer's obvious pull is to the beach, nature's playground, but we also have explored mountains, lakes, and other beautiful spots. Fall in New England is beautiful, with many places where a hike or a bike ride offers panoramic colors in the changing leaves. During the spring, when the snow begins to melt and the temperatures rise, putting on boots and taking a walk somewhere beautiful can call to mind the hope of longer days.

The point is that nature recalls in us something fundamental about ourselves quite different from the standards by which we judge ourselves at work or school. If leisure is, as Pieper suggests, rooted in worship, then the leisure time we make in reconnecting to nature is a result of reminding ourselves that our lives are gifts from God and not primarily to be measured by our usefulness.

Running Around

The opposite of leisure is frenetic, compulsive activity. The fourth-century monk Evagrius, an influential teacher about the spiritual life, described such activity as the result of being driven around by a demon, chasing desires that ultimately do not lead to happiness.[30] We've experienced this kind of activity: we find ourselves running around, shuttling kids here and there, remembering something that must be done, stopping in to pick up one more item in the store, completing one more errand—driven mad by the never-ending to-do list. We come home exhausted, realize there is nothing to eat for dinner, and so on.

What Evagrius pointed to was the phenomenon of disordered desire: that experience of wanting just one more thing that will satisfy a restless soul. He observed that the soul can experience a kind of craving or longing for peace and can be persuaded that it is just out of reach except for this one more thing . . .

Leisure is an antidote for disordered desire, for it is the time of restoration of the soul. In times of leisure, when we suspend our usual drive to get things done, we allow ourselves to reconsider exactly what we believe to be most needful. In the course of a family's life, such pauses are critical, because we live amidst rapidly changing patterns of need. What a child needs at nine can be very different from what she needs at eleven. What must be a family priority when children are all under ten might seem frivolous when they are all teens.

Leisure is a time of discernment, of seeing the big picture with new eyes in order to reconsider why we run around in the first place. For only with the conviction that our running around is purposeful can we enter into it joyfully.

Let us point to one example from our experience. Years ago, our daughters attended the same school, and Dad was in the habit of dropping them off en route to work. The pattern was simple, and it worked well; it was not a great burden. Fast-forward a few years: our oldest daughter was in high school in one town; our middle daughter was in middle school in a second town; and our son was in elementary school in yet a third town. Three kids, three schools, three towns. During this period, both Mom and Dad were involved in drop-offs and pickups; we were constantly running around, ensuring that everyone was where he or she needed to be. The contrast to our earlier situation was striking. But what made the situation tolerable was our deep conviction—which had emerged over many conversations—that each child was in exactly the right school for the right reasons. It was a lot of running around, but it was purposeful.

By contrast, we recall an experience involving a travel sports team. In our experience, the attraction of these teams—which have become major businesses—is rooted in parents' hopes (often unfounded) that their children will develop greater confidence and perhaps earn coveted spots on high school or college teams. We've seen parents wrap entire seasons of their lives around such teams, traveling for weekends or even weeks during summer months, spending hundreds or thousands of dollars on their children's sports. We leave it to others to judge the value of such expenses, but we found that after a couple seasons of one relatively modest travel team experience, enough was enough. We were giving up hours and hours of driving and play time, spending time in gyms far away and eating food on the road. At a certain point, the balance of investment and return seemed to tip away from continuing, so we stopped and regained our weekends.

What we lost during that experience was a significant amount of leisure time. For even though travel sports are a recreational activity—at least for the player—they require that parents become taxi drivers and give up other worthy uses of their time. While that may be a choice for some families, we discerned that for ours, it was not the best one. The experience taught us something about making sure we take time to consider the bigger picture and making a priority of shared leisure time.

Questions for Discernment

Ancient philosophers held that leisure is the reason why we work, the aim of our activity. What might that suggest for your family? "Leisure, for a family, . . . is an interruption in the flow of daily life and a celebration of life for its own sake." As you think of your family life, ask,

- Do you make time to have meals together?
- Does everyone participate in the upkeep of your home in age-appropriate ways? Remember that your family's leisure time means that you can't always be doing all the work!
- Do you make time for shared leisure activities? Having fun together?
- How would you describe the impact of technology (especially screens) on your family life?
- How would you describe the morning routine of getting to work or school? Are there practical changes that might make it easier?

- How would you describe the routine around dinner and bedtime?
- What are some ways you enjoy spending time together on the weekend?
- How do the grown-ups' work schedules impact free time as a family?
- What do you dream of doing with your family if you had the time and money? Are there ways you can schedule smaller experiences of it?
- What is the impact of sports or other activities on your family life?

CHAPTER FOUR

Sabbath

Be still and know that I am God!
—Psalm 46:11

I f authentic leisure arises from worship—that is, an orientation of life that receives it as a precious gift of God to be nurtured—then God's commandment to observe the Sabbath makes sense. For Sabbath is, in this sense, an offering of our leisure time to God first. It is a precious gift for families, a key to reclaiming family time, if we are willing to practice it and thereby come to understand its importance.

In the story of the ten lepers (Luke 17:11-19), Jesus calls to them and tells them to show themselves to the priests. When they do, they discover they are healed. Only one, though, returns to Jesus to express his thanks, leaving Jesus to wonder why the others did not. The story is an image of the way we forget about God, allowing ourselves to be distracted even in the midst of events for which we should be joyful.

What is striking about the story is that the lepers bore their delight in their very skin—their lives were forever changed because of Jesus' healing. Healing from leprosy meant a re-entry into ordinary society and the restoration of relationships with family and friends. It was a chance to leave permanent quarantine and have a normal life again. It ought to have been an occasion for the expression of profound gratitude.

> We must practice—and teach our children—that work does not define us.

And yet our situations are even more profoundly the opportunity to express our gratitude to God. We once did not exist, but the Lord in his goodness has chosen to call us into life, to breathe into us his Spirit and give us the capacity to love others into wholeness. Far greater than healing us of a skin disease is the Lord's gift to us: he has created us in his own image, for a purpose, and given us our years to accomplish it. The call to Sabbath is thus a call to remember that we are the Lord's and that our flesh and our souls bear witness to this great gift.

Practicing Sabbath means, ultimately, that we reclaim all of our family's time for the Lord. Our work and our rest, our play and our recreation, our struggles and our failures, our triumphs and our times of rejoicing—all these belong to the Lord. To paraphrase the words of the psalmist, where can we go to flee from the Lord's presence? (139:7). All of our lives are under the watchful care of the Lord, and so all time is the Lord's time. Practicing Sabbath simply means turning our minds and hearts to him and willfully placing our lives in his hands.

The first practice, then, that we must pass on to our children is to keep the Lord first in all things. "Hear, O Israel! The Lord is our God, the Lord alone!" So begins the powerful prayer known as the *Sh'ma*, the exhortation of Moses to the Israelites after their exodus from Egypt and the gift of the Ten Commandments. "Keep repeating [these words] to your children. Recite them when you are at home and when you are away, when you lie down and when you get up" (Deuteronomy 6:4, 7). Moses wants the Israelites to understand that their lives are precious to God and that their freedom has been secured with great labor. If they are to be a holy nation, they must teach their children how to hold God first in all things.

For us, this exhortation has meant practicing gratitude with our children. For many years, part of our nightly routine has involved reflecting on the past day and beginning with statements of gratitude: "Thank you for our teachers and our friends, thank you for a beautiful sunset, thank you for food and a home to be safe in . . . ," and so on. Even on days marked by sadness or difficulty, we begin with gratitude. As the kids have gotten older, the routine has changed, but we still try to find ways of voicing gratitude: over a meal, at the end of a sports season, or after a day with friends.

Our hope is that the regular practice of gratitude helps form in our kids a sensibility about receiving life as a gift and a readiness to offer it back to God in service. We hope that our practice of celebrating Sabbath at Sunday worship too becomes a formative practice that helps them discern meaning in their lives and a sense of mission—a mission that has a history rooted in the story of Jesus and the Lord's actions throughout salvation history.

A Short History of the Sabbath

We all know the origins of the Sabbath, in the story of God resting from his creation of the world on the seventh day:

> On the seventh day God completed the work he had been doing; he rested on the seventh day from all the work he had undertaken. God blessed the seventh day and made it holy, because on it he rested from all the work he had done in creation. (Genesis 2:2-3)

Modern scholarship suggests that the story comes from a writer of the sixth century BC, representing the priests of Israel after they began to return from exile in Babylon. After generations in exile, one can imagine, Israel was a fragmented community. The recollection of God's creation and the reminder to set aside a day for worship were, for the priestly source, a reminder of who they were as a nation and a summons to keep central the covenant that God had made with their ancestor Abraham.

The third commandment given to Moses describes observance of the Sabbath as a duty to rest:

> Remember the sabbath day—keep it holy. Six days you may labor and do all your work, but the seventh day is a sabbath of the LORD your God. You shall not do any work, either you, your son or your daughter, your male or female slave, your work animal, or the resident alien within your gates. For in

six days the LORD made the heavens and the earth, the sea and all that is in them; but on the seventh day he rested. That is why the LORD has blessed the sabbath day and made it holy. (Exodus 20:8-11)

For centuries, Jews celebrated the Sabbath as both a reminder of creation and as an act of faithfulness to the Law of Moses. Jesus, being a Jew, also observed the holiness of the Sabbath, but he critiqued his contemporaries' observance of it, suggesting that they had become fastidious. Their strict prohibition of any kind of work on the Sabbath, he once taught, prevented even compassionate work such as healing. On one occasion, Jesus asked them, "Is it lawful to do good on the sabbath rather than to do evil, to save life rather than to destroy it?" (Mark 3:4). He meant this question as a test of their understanding of the Sabbath; he went on to heal a man with a withered hand, in violation of the existing law proscribing any sort of work on the Sabbath. Mark goes on to describe his contemporaries resolving then that Jesus must be put to death.

In the Christian era, sabbath observance remained. In the Acts of the Apostles, Luke describes the period following the resurrection as a time of finding a new identity as a people gathered in Jesus' name. In this early period of the Church, the apostles still celebrated the Sabbath in the synagogue (see Acts 13:14, 27, 42, 44). Over time though, Christian celebration of the Sabbath consolidated around the celebration of the Eucharist in house churches (see Acts 2:42-46; 1 Corinthians 11: 17-34).

Eventually Christians celebrated the Sabbath on the day of the resurrection—Sunday, in contrast to the Jewish practice of celebrating Sabbath on Saturday. The second-century apologist Justin Martyr described this practice: "We all gather on the day of the sun, for it is the first day [after the Jewish Sabbath, but also the first day] when God, separating matter from darkness, made the world; and on this same day Jesus Christ our Savior rose from the dead."[31]

Sabbath Today

Today, our celebration of the Mass is a connection to the story of Jesus' institution of the Eucharist and to the centuries of Christian worship that made this practice central to our identity. Observance of the Sabbath is thus a connection to the long story of salvation history: from recollection of God's act of creating the world, to God's giving the Law through Moses, to Jesus' gift to his disciples, to Christian worship of twenty centuries. It is a resistance to what G. K. Chesterton once referred to as a kind of servitude: being "a child of one's own time."[32]

Sabbath is critical for a healthy family life.

Celebration of the Sabbath—and of sabbath rest in general, which we describe as an attitude of treating time as God's first—is critical to family life because it is a regular reminder not to let the demands of the world get in the way of receiving life as a gift.

As we've discussed, it is very easy to fall into patterns of busyness. We are certainly guilty of doing this. With devices issuing regular alerts; with texts, e-mails, phone calls, and people summoning us; with school schedules, sports schedules, music or theater productions, visits with friends, and a hundred other things demanding our attention, it is incredibly easy to become "a child of our own time"—to succumb to the pressure of the moment. And to be sure, it is a kind of servitude: we can really be in thrall to the *now*. We can try to escape it, through mindless flipping through channels, websites, or posts. We can try to outrun it by spending money on vacations or undertaking big projects. But we will never be at rest without Sabbath. *The Catechism of the Catholic Church* puts it this way:

> God's action is the model for human action. If God "rested and was refreshed" on the seventh day, man too ought to "rest" and should let others, especially the poor, "be refreshed." The sabbath brings everyday work to a halt and provides a respite. It is a day of protest against the servitude of work and the worship of money.[33]

Sabbath is thus a reminder of who we are, by recalling that we are God's. We must practice—and teach our children—that work does not define us. It is rather an expression of the persons that God has created us to be, and so it must be rooted in sabbath rest.

It is also important to note that the practice of Sabbath in the ancient world involved allowing the poor to be set free from servitude and to return home. It carried with it a sense of returning everything in creation to its original state in the divine order of the cosmos. The prophet Isaiah gave words to the kind of worship that the Lord demanded of Israel, in contrast to empty observance of religious norms. He demanded a total orientation of people's hearts to justice and mercy:

> Is this not, rather, the fast that I choose:
>> releasing those bound unjustly,
>> untying the thongs of the yoke;
> Setting free the oppressed,
>> breaking off every yoke?
> Is it not sharing your bread with the hungry,
>> bringing the afflicted and the homeless into your house;
> Clothing the naked when you see them,
>> and not turning your back on your own flesh?
> Then your light shall break forth like the dawn,
>> and your wound shall quickly be healed;
> Your vindication shall go before you,
>> and the glory of the LORD shall be your rear guard.
> (Isaiah 58:6-8)

Following Isaiah's logic means not merely making worship an isolated practice, but rather allowing it to so transform our vision of the world that our lives become more and more oriented toward building the kind of kingdom where those bound are released, the hungry have food, the homeless have homes, and the naked are clothed. In short, there is a direct connection between Sabbath and the works of mercy.

It is possible to read these injunctions as part of a mission statement for family life. For as parents, we have been called to service: we give food to hungry children; we give them homes, feed them, and release them from the bondage of their untutored desires. We are preparing them for the kingdom of God. Further, with the Lord's help, our service reaches beyond our walls into our communities, where we teach our children service by encouraging them to do it: participating in food drives or going to work at a food pantry or homeless shelter, contributing to clothing drives or working at a facility that serves area shelters, reaching out to elderly neighbors or babysitting for friends who have lost spouses, and many other ways.

The practice of Sabbath is about keeping one foot in eternity and another foot in the ordinary cycle of life that we experience on a daily basis.

Over our family's life, we've experienced many such ways of connecting Sabbath and service, and every now and again, we discern signs of how these practices are influencing our children's view of the world. They are learning, we hope, that Sabbath is the practice of withdrawing for a time to call to mind God's desire that the world be a place where there is room for all the members of his family.

One of our children, while still a tween, would occasionally wonder what might happen if we made a lot of money. "Would you give it to the poor?" Our answer was consistent: "Part of it, yes." For while we had never explicitly discussed the biblical concept of tithing—a practice related to Sabbath, in the sense that it involved offering one's first fruits to the Lord (see Deuteronomy 14:22-29)—our child had intuited that our lives were dedicated to serving God in all things and that serving the poor was central to that mission.

Sabbath as Making Room

The writers of the New Testament describe the way that people responded to Jesus by either making room for his words or shaking their heads and turning away. The Greek verb is *choreo*, meaning "to accept," "to receive," or "to have room." When Jesus begins teaching on marriage and points to the way that God intended it to be in the beginning, he observes, "Not all can accept [this] word" (Matthew 19:11). The teaching about the permanence of marriage, he recognizes, is difficult in a world where some men callously dismiss their wives in order to marry someone else. What he implies is that "accepting" God's word means fundamentally reorienting your life—rejecting the easy solutions offered by society and trusting in the Lord's often difficult path.

Similarly, in John's Gospel, Jesus accuses some of his peers of resting too easily in their assumption that being descendants of Abraham is proof of their being children of God.

He says, "You are trying to kill me, because my word has no room among you" (John 8:37). Jesus' word "has no room" because they believe that their lives are fine as they are, needing no reorientation (the biblical word is "repentance") to more fully embrace God's call to love and service.

A related word that the New Testament writers use is *anachoreo*, which can be translated "to withdraw" or "to leave," but its roots suggest the image of "making room for each one." New Testament scholar Bonnie Thurston suggests that Jesus' times of withdrawal from activity in order to focus on prayer were meant to "make room" for the people that the Father placed before him.[34] He withdrew in order that he might return.[35] For us who follow Jesus, Sabbath is similar: it is a recentering of our lives on the Lord in order that we too might make room in our lives for the ways that the Lord calls us to ever greater love.

Living as we do according to school schedules—both because of the kids' school schedules and because of Dad's academic year schedule—we have developed a certain pattern of withdrawal and return. Semesters have a beginning, middle, and end, and then a time for rest. Between terms, there are periods of vacation, when the board is wiped clean and everyone starts afresh. There is a certain rhythm to the academic year. It mirrors the liturgical year, with its annual beginning in Advent, its fallow period of ordinary time, and its long Lent, yielding to the beautiful Easter season and then again ordinary time.

These rhythms, like those of the agricultural seasons that gave rise to the marking of time on calendars, make it easy to fall into patterns of withdrawal and return. What we notice as a consequence is that periods of withdrawal call forth big-picture thinking. Rather than getting caught in the minutiae of daily life with its pressing demands, we have the opportunity to ask the bigger questions: How is our life going? What is most important to us at this stage? How have our children grown? What are our areas of growth or decline?

> Developing a habit of prayer is available to anyone, anytime, by just stopping for a moment and praying as the Lord leads you, even if you've been away from prayer or have no idea how to do it well.

To carry the metaphor that the New Testament authors suggested, periods of Sabbath allow us to make room for the people in our lives who call forth our love and attention. We see the fruits of our practice of thankfulness, for example, when through our giving thanks, we immediately turn our minds to those who lack the things for which we have just expressed thanks. After a hard day at work, for example, an expression of gratitude for work immediately becomes a plea for those who are out of work. Gratitude for even a messy home becomes hope for those who are homeless. And so on.

By making room in our hearts for others, Sabbath is thus also a period of discernment. Discernment, the practice of listening to the desires of our hearts for signs of God's grace,[36] becomes attuned in periods of Sabbath, for it is during those times that we recall that we belong to the Lord and find our joy in serving the purposes for which he has equipped us.

Sabbath and the Family Life Cycle

We are convinced that the practice of Sabbath is critical for a healthy family life. We mean this in the specific sense of practicing worship on Sunday, as well as in the more general sense of taking time to reorient our lives on the service of God through practices of prayer and reflection.

This conviction came home to us in a conversation we had the other day. We were out walking our dog and ran into a neighbor whom we hadn't seen for a few months. It was a good chance to catch up and learn how his three children, similar in age to ours, were doing. One had begun college and was looking forward to a semester abroad; another was considering his next move after graduating from high school. The third was about to begin high school. Our short conversation reminded us of how quickly time passes with children: it seemed only last week that his kids were still small. Now, it seemed, they were in the midst of life changes, and he and his wife were beginning to imagine what life would be like as empty nesters.

So too for us, we realized! The family life cycle moves swiftly from infancy to adulthood and seems to move more quickly as children age. The author of Ecclesiastes put his finger on this constant in human experience:

One generation departs and another generation
   comes,
  but the world forever stays.
The sun rises and the sun sets;
  then it presses on to the place where it rises.
(Ecclesiastes 1:4-5)

For us, the practice of Sabbath is about keeping one foot in eternity and another foot in the ordinary cycle of life that we experience on a daily basis. Later in the book of Ecclesiastes, the author describes the human heart as something that the Lord has designed for eternity: "God has made everything appropriate to its time, but has put the timeless into [human] hearts" (3:11).

Perhaps you too have had moments of recognizing the passage of time in your children's lives. You are going through clothes and realize that your child has outgrown them. You remember events where she wore that dress or when he took that school picture. You shop for school supplies and can't believe that your baby is now in middle school. You look at pictures from a family vacation and realize that it's already been five years since you experienced it. You see a former teacher at the grocery store and remember that your child hasn't been in her class for many years now. All such experiences are reminders that our lives pass quickly and that it is important not to allow the speed of daily life to get in the way of savoring the precious time you have together.

Sabbath is the daily and weekly practice of placing all time in the hands of the Lord so that he might sanctify your family's life and create in you a heart that cherishes it. It is a concrete manifestation of a spirituality of time, which might be described as an attentiveness to living in the present moment, mindful that each moment is also at the same time rooted in the eternity of the Lord.

This moment is a gift of the Lord.

So is this one.

So is this one.

Sabbath practices—both Sunday worship and regular prayer and reflection on a daily basis—allow us to enter mindfully into our daily lives so that we may live them with the serenity that comes from serving the Lord's purposes. It is a form of sacrifice—of "holy offering," as the word's etymology suggests. When we offer our time and our attention to God, we freely give to the Lord our very lives and ask him to sanctify them. This sacrifice is an act of freedom, oriented toward achieving the ends for which the Lord has given us life. Josef Pieper states it well:

> The Christian conception of sacrifice is not concerned with the suffering involved *qua* suffering, it is not primarily concerned with the toil and the worry and with the difficulty, but

with salvation, with the fullness of being, and thus ultimately with the fullness of happiness: "The end and the norm of discipline is happiness."[37]

What Pieper is pointing to is the fact that any form of sacrifice means giving up something, but that the Christian conception of sacrifice involves the recognition that our actions are meaningful not only in themselves but also in the larger end for which we do them. We all know this on an intuitive level as parents: we sacrifice daily for our children because we have a vision of the kinds of persons they will become with our love and care. Sabbath sacrifices—going to Mass, insuring our children's religious education, daily time spent in prayer—are not only about the actions by which we connect our lives to the designs God has for our lives but also regular reminders that the Lord calls us to missions beyond what we imagine in the present moment.

As we write this, we are in the midst of the Christmas season, which is in itself a kind of sabbath season for us. For in addition to being a holy season celebrating Christ's birth, it is a time of school vacation. Our schedules slow down, and we have the opportunity to spend more time as a family. Our Christmas traditions connect us to the long story of our family life and summon rich memories.

Buying and decorating the Christmas tree, to use one example, is an activity that spans decades. Going to select a tree calls to mind the many years we spent living in Indiana, Pennsylvania, "the Christmas tree capital of the world," where every year we could wander around beautiful tree farms to find the perfect Fraser fir. We think of photos from one year when there were many inches of snow on the ground; our daughters were still very small and loved trudging through the powder to find a tree. Decorating the tree means looking through decades' worth of ornaments: some from Nana's family; some, memories from trips we've taken; some, memories of places we've lived or worked; some homemade by children when they were younger. Decorating the tree is the opportunity to talk about family memories, to tell stories of good times and hard times and even times before our children even existed.

The Christmas season is a reminder that the Lord "has put the timeless into [human] hearts"(Ecclesiastes 3:11). It helps us to keep one foot in eternity and one foot in daily life, and so draws us to worship. Of course, the liturgies during this time of year make it easy: there is a sense of joy in the air as our parish choirs sing carols and hymns that date back centuries, connecting us to the long story of the Church's origins in the birth of Christ. This year, at the Christmas Eve vigil Mass, our parish was packed, standing room only, with families gathered with loved ones visiting from far-flung places. Extended families were happy at seeing siblings, aunts, uncles, cousins, and grandparents, and they brought their palpable joy into the celebration of the liturgy.

Very often, though, celebration of liturgy feels more like a sacrifice than what we experience during the Christmas season. Many families struggle to make Mass going a weekly priority. As a director of family ministries at our parish, Sue has seen many examples of families who experience great difficulty celebrating Mass together, whether due to work schedules, differences of belief between parents, or simple exhaustion.

Nevertheless, weekly Mass going remains one of the Church's "precepts," or rules binding all Catholics.[38] Rather than seeing it as an arbitrary law, though, we see it as rooted in something fundamental about our lives—rather like rules about nutrition, which similarly are about connecting behaviors to basic needs. The Church prescribes weekly Sabbath because God has prescribed it; he has built into our very humanness the need for connection to him and to one another.

> It is important not to allow the speed of daily life get in the way of savoring the precious time you have together.

Let us be very frank and recognize that many of our peers spend Sunday morning exercising, or going to some sporting event, or relaxing at home. More people do *not* go to church on a regular basis than do. Sabbath worship is indeed a sacrifice. Sometimes it can feel like a chore, especially when children dig in their heels and do not want to go. We've dealt with that problem over many years, from toddlerhood to teenage years. There is no easy solution, but for us, one way to moderate the problem is to establish the definite habit of Mass going every week, without fail. Our kids understand that the weekend revolves around planning for Mass, for they have experienced it without fail for their entire lives.

For our part, encouraging them to understand *what* they are doing and *why* they are doing it has changed over the years. As children, they attended religious education classes, which in our parish has always involved primarily parental instruction. During the Mass itself, our children have used *MagnifiKid!* which our parish orders in bulk. It's a child-friendly weekly guide to the Mass, so kids can follow along and understand the readings.

Frequently, our parish offers a children's Liturgy of the Word, so that kids can experience an age-appropriate reading and reflection on the readings for the day. Often we'll make reference to the readings, either in the car on the way to Mass or at breakfast afterward. We hope to convey something of the meaning in these texts, perhaps as they relate to the time of the liturgical year or to an important theme like healing, prayer, or patient trust in the Lord.

There are a number of ways we try to make connections between our daily life and the Church's liturgy. Obvious examples are the use of symbols like the Advent wreath or the Lenten rice bowl for collecting money for the poor. The seasons of Advent and Lent, with their counting down of days, make it easy. During ordinary time, our prayer will often be more spontaneous.

We have, over the years, experimented with more formal ways of praying as a family, and we have friends and family who do different things, whether a daily decade of the Rosary or some other formal prayer. For us, especially as our kids are getting older, daily prayer may be at meals or bedtime. We will sometimes pause at midday and pray the Angelus.

As Catholics, we have a deep "tool kit" of prayer—any time and any number of ways of praying can be deployed to try to draw family back to the fundamental place of Sabbath. We have found that a certain flexibility, based on kids' ages and dispositions, is more likely to succeed than a one-size-fits-all approach to family prayer. More important, we are convinced that developing a habit of prayer is available to anyone, anytime, by just stopping for a moment and praying as the Lord leads you, even if you've been away from prayer or have no idea how to do it well.

Questions for Discernment

1. Our lives are an opportunity to express thanks to God. Living with gratitude is key to happiness. In what ways do you encourage your family members to practice the art of gratitude? Do you model a grateful attitude within your family? If not, how can you improve in this regard?

2. Sabbath is the practice of taking time away from the busyness of life to express gratitude and praise to God. It is the third commandment too, because it is fundamental to our ability to orient our lives toward leisure. God tells us to rest because he made us for leisure. Examine the ways your family observes sabbath rest. Do you see room for improvement? What activities can you move to another day?

3. For Catholics, celebration of the Sabbaths means going to Mass, but there is also a connection between worship and service. Do you treat worship as an isolated activity, or are you helping your children see the link between worship and service? In what specific ways can you do this?

4. A way of conceiving of Sabbath is according to the Greek notion of "making room" for everyone but also withdrawing for a time in order for that to happen. How do you balance the notion of withdrawing with the need to be attentive to your family and to actively plan at least some sabbath activities?

5. "The practice of Sabbath is about keeping one foot in eternity and another foot in the ordinary cycle of life that we experience on a daily basis." It sanctifies everyday life and helps us to see God present in all we do as a family. Do you experience the Sabbath in this way? Does your family? If not, what can you do to foster a greater awareness of God's presence in your family, flowing from your sabbath practice?

6. Regular prayers and devotions help orient us toward Sabbath on a daily basis. How can you help your children develop age-appropriate ways to pray? Do you encourage your children to practice daily prayer on their own, not just as a family activity?

CHAPTER FIVE

Times and Seasons

We must slow down to a human tempo and we'll begin to have time to listen. . . . But for this we have to experience time in a new way. . . . The reason why we don't take time is a feeling that we have to keep moving. This is a real sickness. Today time is a commodity, and for each one of us time is mortgaged. . . . We must approach the whole idea of time in a new way. We live in the fullness of time. Every moment is God's own good time, his kairos.
—Thomas Merton[39]

My times are in your hand.
—cf. Psalm 31:16

We have always cherished the last days of summer as they creep toward the beginning of the new school year. The long days and long, drooping evenings will soon, we know, be behind us. Perhaps there will be a fire in the backyard in the new fire pit we set up, hoping to encourage kids and their friends to linger there while toasting marshmallows and suspending, for a while, the tittering that happens over their devices. Perhaps we will make a run to the local Dairy Queen and have soft-serve, allowing the frozen swirls to drip lightly on our knuckles as we quickly slurp up the melt where the ice cream meets the cone. Or perhaps we are emptying the van after a day trip to the beach; there is sand on boogie boards and on our feet as we scramble to rinse ourselves off and unload the car, hoping to catch a quick shower before cozying up for a movie night at home or at the drive-in.

> Time is not only about getting things accomplished and marking days off a calendar; it is also about seeking the Lord's hand active in creation, if we but pause long enough.

There is a sense of urgency to this relaxation, paradoxically: everyone knows that within a few days the schedule will begin again, with early morning wake-ups, gathering of school supplies, fussing over appearances, (hopefully) eating breakfast, and heading out the door. Dad will head one way with two of the kids, and Mom will head a different way with child number three. Then both will be off to work, negotiating who is picking up whom and which child will be going which way with which friend before returning home for homework and dinner.

There are times, and there are seasons. Most of us understand the difference between the daily grind and the rich times of which memories are made, and most of us understand that memories can be made within a few hours and last a lifetime. Most of us, too, wrestle with a desire to make meaningful memories and the practical reality that there is a lot that needs to get done. We understand that reclaiming family time is about both reclaiming our family and reclaiming time itself. We can learn much about how to do that by considering a biblical theology of time.

A Biblical Theology of Time

We live our lives taking our cues from the culture around us, and therefore few of us give much thought to how we understand time. Time is just what passes on a daily basis. But everyone has had those experiences of time standing still. Maybe we are immersed in some enjoyable activity that makes time seem to evaporate, so that we suddenly realize we've spent three hours that felt like ten minutes. Or maybe we are waiting in line at a store or an office, and ten minutes feels like three hours. We experience a certain "plasticity" of time—that is, we understand how we ourselves mold and shape our experience of time based on what's going on inside of us: our emotions, our activities, our desires.

For those of us who study the ancient world, what quickly becomes apparent is that time is not simply a given, an objective fact that can be measured ever-so precisely by more and more sophisticated chronometers. Today we live in a world governed, in many ways, by technology—that is, by the things we human beings make: electric lights that extend our working hours, computers and phones that tie us to the office 24/7/365, cars that extend the distance we travel on a daily basis, TVs that entertain us while we retreat from public spaces, and so on. We have become disconnected from nature and from one another, and we often collapse into the craving that arises from the experience of our most immediate desires.

For us, time is remarkably plastic, because in many ways, we can manipulate it and strangle it, monetize it and sell it. On the other hand, we can cultivate it and share it, discern how to use it well to serve greater goods. Our control over time comes with a high cost: by using it badly, we can experience alienation and loneliness, but by using it well, we can experience connection and a sense of mission in the world.

The ancient world, by contrast, was governed by the natural order: sunrises and sunsets, tides and phases of the moon, plantings and harvests, community gatherings and festivals. For the ancients, time was an objective reality, and human beings were utterly subject to it. To use one example, the name given to the Greek Titan Cronus—father to the Olympian gods Zeus, Hera, and others—may have come from *chronos*, the root of our word *chronology*, meaning "measured time."[40]

According to the Roman orator Cicero, Cronus was so named because he governed the "course and revolution of periods and times."[41] Time was, for Cicero and many others, the realm of the gods, and human beings were but players in a vast cosmic drama over which they had little control.

The ancient Israelite theology of time shared some similarity with that of the Greeks and Romans in that time was a constant in the order of creation and governed by the hand of God. We've seen how the very notion of Sabbath emerged in Israel as a result of recognizing God's rest after creation.

Sabbath called for a community response to a larger reality—that everything in the cosmos, including time itself, came from God and was ordered to God's purposes.

Today we may retain some of that sensibility, especially during times of feast. Consider the Christian celebration of the Eucharist and its roots in the Jewish celebration of Passover. Every year Jews celebrate the Passover at the seder meal, during which participants recall and make present the story of Moses leading the Israelites out of Egypt. Similarly, Christians recall and make present the Last Supper between Jesus and his disciples, who themselves may have been celebrating a seder meal.[42] Such celebrations are interruptions in our normal experience of time; we make ourselves present to the past, as it were. Or consider the seasons of Christmas and the Easter Triduum, when we condense and stretch time. In early December, we celebrate the Immaculate Conception, when St. Anne conceives a sinless Mary in her womb; and seventeen days later, we celebrate Christmas, when Mary herself gives birth to Jesus. At the liturgy of the Easter Vigil, we stand next to the Father and watch history itself unfold in the readings. We hear stories that cover the entirety of salvation history, from God's creation of the world to Christ's rising from death to life.

Celebrations such as these remind us that time is not only about getting things accomplished and marking days off a calendar; it is also about seeking the Lord's hand active in creation, if we but pause long enough to recall that he died in order to redeem it.

The biblical writers describe time in ways that can inform the way we approach family life. Lest we get too caught up in daily chores, the texts remind us that the Lord has established time itself (Genesis 1:14); he has ordered the nations and their time upon the earth (Daniel 2:21; Acts 17:26).

The Lord's designs prevail (Proverbs 16:4; Isaiah 46:10) because he is not limited by time (Psalm 90:4), nor does he grow tired (Isaiah 40:28). He will bring about the consummation of history when Jesus returns (Ephesians 1:9-10; 1 Timothy 6:15). He is the "Alpha and the Omega, . . . the beginning and the end" of all time (Revelation 22:13).

> Prayer is the daily practice of switching lenses: it is the regular practice of adapting our vision more and more to that of Jesus.

Even though we experience time as passing (Psalm 144:4; James 4:14), still, our well-being is in the hands of the Lord (Psalm 31:16, as noted at the beginning of this chapter). Now, according to Luke, is a time "acceptable to the Lord" (4:19) because of Jesus' coming to announce good news to the poor. Now, according to Luke's traveling companion Paul, is "a very acceptable time; behold, now is the day of salvation" (2 Corinthians 6:2). What this means, at least on the face of things, is quite simple: now is the acceptable time to reclaim family life. The Lord has sanctified all time; nothing else is necessary— not the end of the school year, not the next vacation period, not the next free weekend. Now!

What emerges as an essential dimension in Jesus' preaching is a sense of expectant hope, that the time to change our lives and our approach to time is right in front of us. As we saw last chapter, Jesus' appeal to "make room for each one" (*anachoreo*) has a certain urgency to it—it tells us parents, "Don't waste time! Your children are young for but a brief moment!" Time is not only about a steady march toward adulthood and old age, it is also about taking advantage of the limited opportunities we have to experience a foretaste of the heavenly banquet. It is about inviting the Lord to act in our daily lives, transforming them into opportunities to see the good, true, and beautiful amidst the mundane.

Kairos Time

One of the biblical Greek words for time is *kairos*, which is often translated as some variation of "acceptable time," as we saw in Paul's exhortation to the Corinthians above. *Kairos* is about opportunity, while often *chronos* is about measuring time. The desire to reclaim family time is ultimately about developing the practice of living in what Thomas Merton described as "God's own good time, his *kairos.*" It is about stepping out of the usual chronology of our days—that is, whatever appears in our schedule books or calendaring apps—and making room for spontaneity, discovery, and wonder with our families.

Anyone with small children or grandchildren certainly can remember experiences of "wasting time" with children and how wonderful such experiences can be. The imaginative worlds that young people inhabit can be hilarious, insightful, creative, surprising—the list goes on. You cannot rush a child's experience of the world any more than you can make a flower bloom by yanking it up from the ground. Family life ought to have a natural rhythm of kairos: an attentiveness to God's presence amidst the noise and clutter.

We would be lying if we told you that we've mastered this practice, even though we hold it as a good that we strive for daily. For us, seeking kairos is about freedom: the freedom to live in God's time rather than the packed, hurried time of our own making. God's time is, to use an allegory, what existed in the garden of Eden: a place of serene receptivity to the good things that God has made. Seeking kairos is about being willing to suspend ourselves from whatever the immediate objective of the moment is: getting ready for school, finishing a project, doing chores—and simply attending to the revelation of the moment.

Just last evening we had an experience of such a kairos. We were going about our usual evening routine of making dinner and helping the kids with homework. With several demands on our attention, we were beginning to feel a little stressed and started watching the clock for when dinner would be ready and when the bedtime routine had to happen in order for everyone to get adequate sleep for the next day. Present were all the usual stressors: concern about getting food into bodies before the kids got crabby, concern about making sure homework was getting done properly, concern about making sure everyone did his or her fair share and no fights broke out about who wasn't helping, concern about carving out some time for ourselves to get work done that had not been completed during the day, and so on. On this evening, we discovered that one of the kids had missed several assignments over the past month, and so we had to negotiate a way to have a serious conversation.

That conversation was hard for our child, dredging up fears and insecurities. But it also offered an opportunity—a kairos—for us to express our love and constant support. We shared big-picture lessons about life, about working hard toward goals, about discerning God's voice amidst the many things that call for our attention. It was, in short, an important moment of bonding and sharing how much we supported and loved our child through difficulties in school.

> Festivity is not about ignoring the reality of life—that's why we find some forms of partying to run at cross-purposes to real festivity.

It would have been very easy to miss this kairos, and earlier in our married life, we might have done so. But we have come to value various practices that enhance our ability to pause from chronos time in order to dwell, when occasions present themselves, in kairos time. We've already dealt at length with the primary practice of Sabbath, which orients our lives toward discerning God's plans in all things. The complementary practice, which unfolds in day-to-day habits, is known in Christian tradition as contemplation.

Contemplation

In several places throughout the Bible, the writers point to the ways that people often go through life without really understanding the meaning of what they experience. The prophet Isaiah describes God's lament for his people: "They do not know, do not understand; / their eyes are too clouded to see, / their minds, to perceive" (44:18). Matthew describes Jesus trying mightily to make people understand the kingdom of God in their midst, devoting several parables to the ways that people tend to miss what God is doing among them. Jesus says, "This is why I speak to them in parables, because 'they look but do not see and hear but do not listen or understand'" (Matthew 13:13). Again and again, we see similar comments. People are blind to the reality of God right underneath their noses.[43]

Consider the past twenty-four hours. No doubt you, like us, can point to things that got done, from mundane things like eating a meal or going shopping to more meaningful things like having a phone conversation with a family member. We have mental to-do lists—and sometimes written or digital ones—which tend to guide our daily choices. If you're like us, what you see on a daily basis are the "necessary" activities, the things you perceive as important for the daily functioning of your life. You see the world primarily through a lens we might call "utility"—that is, a lens that allows us first to see what is useful.

Now, consider the past twenty-four hours through a different lens, one that we'll call "relationship." Through this lens, you can pay attention to the ways that you interacted with people to build relationship with them. Pay attention to the key relationships in your life, especially those in your immediate family, and ask what the interactions with those people were like. What did you communicate? What did you seek to understand? In what ways did you demonstrate your love and care for them?

Let's apply a third lens, which we'll call "grace." As you consider the past twenty-four hours, when did you discern signs of God's grace? When, for example, did you experience yourself practicing generosity toward someone? When did you feel loved? When did you recognize something beautiful, whether in nature or in something made by human beings—a song, a work of art, a book, or something else? When did you notice yourself responding to an injustice or feeling sympathy for someone going through a hard time? When were you moved to pray or express a hope to God?

There are many lenses we can use to look at the world, but the important practice is switching out the one we use most often—utility. Contemplation, we'll suggest, arises when we move away from seeing the world through the lens of utility and start seeing it in ways suggested by Jesus' parables and actions. Prayer is the daily practice of switching lenses: it is the regular practice of adapting our vision more and more to that of Jesus.

In contrast to our common way of seeing the world, which one writer suggested is "an act of aggression," seeking to control the world we live in and manipulate it toward our purposes,[44] contemplation is a posture of receptivity to the world that God has made and has invited us to help shape toward his plans. Practices of prayer, mindfulness, reflection, and journaling—including the Ignatian practice of the Examen, a prayer of recalling the past day, which we recommend for families in our book *Six Sacred Rules for Families*—cultivate in us the habit of contemplation.

"Happiness," writes St. Thomas Aquinas, "consists in contemplation," for it is a participation in the divine life.[45] Thomas, though, writing in the thirteenth century, believed that contemplative life was reserved for those who enter a religious order, distinguishing that life from the more active life of families. To be sure, there is a vocation to contemplative life, a call that God issues to some who will choose lives of prayer in a cloister or monastery. Yet we are convinced that it is possible and, in some sense, necessary for active people—those called to the vocation of family life—to develop habits of contemplation that center their busy lives on the Lord's invitation to relationship.

Thomas exhorts those engaged in a contemplative life to "give to others the fruits of contemplation."[46] This exhortation—a motto of the Dominican order, of which he was an influential early member—suggests for us an approach to the balance between prayer and the busyness of family life. Through contemplation, we become attuned to the daily workings of grace—God "laboring" (as St. Ignatius of Loyola suggested) in his creation, moving it toward the good.[47] Developing the habit of seeing God laboring in the daily lives of our families is about developing the vision to "see and understand" in a manner suggested by Jesus.

Giving to others the fruits of contemplation is nothing less than sharing our most authentic selves with others—including our children—and also sharing with them a life compass well calibrated toward the divine life. It is about daily attempts to switch out the lens of utility for lenses more apt for seeing the way God sees. It is about what St. Paul described as the "fruit of the Spirit": "love, joy, peace, patience, kindness, generosity, faithfulness, gentleness, self-control" (Galatians 5:22-23). It is resisting the temptation to hurry through tasks, taking time to listen to a child, even in the midst of a tantrum. It is bringing children along to serve at a homeless shelter or at the home of a neighbor and reflecting on the experience before bedtime. It is engaging kids' questions about politics or social issues, gently nudging them to critique what they hear around school. It is about planning a day with one of your children who needs some Mom time.

It is about recognizing in kids' complaints the seeds of some insecurity or fear and returning to it when there is time for conversation. It is about interrupting your day when a child wants time outside, and the sun happens to be shining. It is about riding a bike together in freezing winter weather, just because that's what will give your newly adopted son a sense of excitement about the new home he lives in.

The Carmelite William McNamara describes contemplation as "a long loving look at the real."[48] That is an apt description of what parenthood summons from us: eyes to see not only what is most evident but also the deep meanings unfolding before us as our children navigate the mysteries that are their very selves. What is necessary for kairos time is not necessarily time off of work or vacations away from home. Rather, what is necessary is contemplation, which opens us to the possibility of finding kairos moments throughout the day. Now is an opportune time.

Festivity

One of the most delightful contemplative practices is festivity. From the ordinary family dinner to birthday parties, adoption days, and holidays, festive celebrations are kairos times. Festivity can be thought of as a kind of spiritual practice, inasmuch as it gives us the opportunity to suspend the usual demands of our lives and simply enjoy the goodness of one another. It calls for a certain renunciation, a certain ascesis, defined as the willingness to give up something in order to achieve a spiritual benefit. The paradox, of course, is that unlike other forms of ascesis like fasting or abstaining from meat—practices proper to other seasons of the year—festivity calls for the renunciation of utility in favor of extravagance.

Jesus himself gave the example *par excellence* at the wedding at Cana (John 2:1-12). It was Mary who exhorted Jesus to perform his first miracle in order to enhance festivity. Mary, ever the mother, possessed a wisdom that Jesus himself had yet to discern: that a family celebration may well be the closest we get to the heavenly banquet. She understood what the bridegroom was feeling: a sense that the party was likely to wind down as the wine ran out. Perhaps she knew that the young man did not come from means, and struggled even to provide food for his guests so that they might share his joy.

Jesus was still a young man, and he certainly desired his Father's will in all things, yet he did not then rank festivity as his highest concern. Mary, though, saw an opportunity, a kairos: changing the water into wine so that the gladness of the guests might not be cut short. Perhaps she knew the sentiment expressed by another man named Jesus, son of Eleazar, son of Sira: "Gladness of heart is the very life of a person, / and cheerfulness prolongs his days."[49] She urged Jesus to take another look at the way that this festivity might be a sacrament of divine gladness.

Our hearts are very often like that of Jesus before the urging of his mother: good, holy, well-intentioned, yet removed from the immediate moment. The summons to festivity is indeed sacramental, in the sense that it calls us to invite the Lord to sanctify the ordinary people and places where we set aside time simply to be in one another's presence. The kitchen, the site of so much of our daily labor—cutting and chopping, cooking and washing—becomes the locus of holy gladness. The living area, where we do laundry and where we are constantly picking up discarded shoes and socks, becomes a kind of sanctuary where, in an acceptable time, festivity unfolds. Our ordinary spaces become holy places where we build memories that we will share in years to come.

What we have noticed in times of festivity—summer vacations with extended family or Christmas gatherings with people dear to us—is that they are times when our kids return to themselves. To put it crassly, we like being around them more. Gone, for a time, are the usual preoccupations with appearance and the social dramas that push and pull on a daily basis. With adequate sleep, no stress from homework, and time to do what they enjoy, they show a greater willingness to be in the moment, perhaps playing a game with cousins or friends or talking with a relative who can't believe how big they are getting.

Perhaps it is because festivity often coincides with holidays that mark the passage of years; we connect in our minds the memories from past years' celebrations and recognize the ways our children have grown and changed over the years. Perhaps it is because festivity offers the chance to draw families closer together, saying effectively, "These are the people you will celebrate with many years from now, long after most of your current friends have moved on with their lives." To be sure, that is a message we sometimes voice, particularly now as our children are in their teen years and likely to be drawn away from family toward friends. But festivity issues a reminder of the transitoriness of life, even as it draws us to celebrate the life we have now.

In recent years, times of festivity have not been without difficulty. For even though festivity allows us to take a step back from daily life, doing so can also bring home the difference between the life we have and the life we want. Our family has had to wrestle with sickness, job insecurity, strained relationships, and death, to name a few. Festivity is not about ignoring the reality of life—that's why we find some forms of partying to run at cross-purposes to real festivity. Rather, it's about choosing to find kairos even in the midst of difficulty, to offer to the Lord our hopes and our desires even in the midst of the difficulty. Festivity is, in this sense, a kind of hopeful expectation, a microcosm of the hope expressed by the entire pilgrim people of God anticipating Christ's return. "You changed my mourning into dancing; / you took off my sackcloth / and clothed me with gladness," writes the psalmist (30:12), expressing the hope of all God's people.

Practical Steps

Like all forms of Christian spirituality, practicing contemplation and developing habits of kairos time in our families involve forms of what are called in Christian tradition by different names: renunciation, detachment, indifference. All these terms refer to a basic dynamic: following Christ means sometimes doing things differently from others around us. Renunciation is saying no to certain things that may be common or popular. Many parents do this on a regular basis, whether it means setting limits on their kids' device use, teaching them about the dangers of drugs and alcohol, or withholding permission to go to a certain party.

Detachment, similarly, is about choosing not to get attached to certain ways of thinking or acting that compromise the ability to live full lives. We wrote about one example in *Six Sacred Rules for Families*: namely, the drive for success that we see taking a major toll on family life. When success becomes an idol, time is easily reduced to utility, and kairos time evaporates. Indifference, far from being a "whatever" attitude (as colloquial use would have it), is a posture of readiness to go wherever God leads us. It is a rich theme in the Christian tradition that points to a certain spiritual freedom and a refusal to be enslaved to what "everyone thinks."

Here we will suggest several strategies for encouraging contemplative practices that allow for the discovery of kairos time. We've already pointed to one practical idea: have parties! Any way that families remove themselves from the flow of utility in order to celebrate is an opportunity for thanksgiving. Every family has a natural rhythm of celebration. In addition to the usual feasts in the liturgical calendar—Christmas and Easter, for example—there are days unique to each family. Birthdays or adoption days are opportunities to give particular focus to one person's blessing to the family. These events need not be expensive, but they offer an opportunity to be thoughtful. Anniversaries—whether of your wedding, or of the day you first moved into your house, or of a memorable achievement— are opportunities to dwell within the plasticity of kairos time. Similar examples are the first day of school, the first day of summer vacation, or civic holidays like the Fourth of July or Martin Luther King Day.

It may be worth taking time at the beginning of a year or a semester to plan out festivities, giving them priority in your mind and in your planning. Some years we've done this well, others not so much—but when we do it well, the fruits are constant. We've gotten better at planning our summers, for example, in large part because it's the time of year when everyone is freer than during the school year. We try to make planning major holidays, birthdays, and adoption days a priority too, and our kids understand that those celebrations are sacrosanct, in the sense of being off-limits for planning alone activities—even as they get older and enjoy their growing autonomy.

Consider your children's ages, and think about what pace of family celebrations makes sense. Perhaps monthly you find some weekend day set aside to spend leisure time together, rather than in separate activities. At different times of our lives, we've planned beach trips, ski trips, trips to visit extended family, and so on. We observe that there is something about getting out of the usual space of our home that can encourage an attitude of kairos—as though there is a kind of kairos space as much as there is kairos time. If home is a place kids associate with work, then go to a park, museum, or restaurant. It need not be an expensive proposition—we have found many ways over the years to find kairos even when the budget is tight.

Be willing to take some risks planning adventures. We've mentioned how we've developed a tradition of allowing Dad to choose what happens on Father's Day, for example, and we've experimented with allowing our kids (at a certain age) to decide how we spend our family time together. Often they will default to watching a movie at home, which can be fun, but we've also tried to offer several more interesting alternatives that they might choose from: "Would you rather go into the city to enjoy a picnic by the water or go bike riding along the rail trail and get pizza afterward?" Our emphasis is on having fun together and creating memories. A small investment of time researching opportunities in your area will give you a tool kit of ideas to deploy at various times of the year.

> Sports schedules are becoming like an invasive species over family life; our response has been to engage moderately, but to be ready to say no.

On a daily basis, there are practices that we have found help us to cultivate kairos. Some are as simple as introducing moments of private or family prayer, which keep us mindful of the Lord's call to be good parents. Perhaps it's a short time reading the Scriptures first thing in the morning or right before bed. Recently we've begun introducing the Angelus— the five-minute prayer often said at noon—when people are around during the weekend. We set an alarm on our phones and pause from whatever we're doing, with whomever we're doing it, and pray this micro liturgy of the Incarnation. Pauses before meals for prayer are a regular practice, as are blessings of individual children on birthdays, adoption days, the first day of school, days before a big test, or other occasions.

Planning weekends is a skill we have not mastered and probably never will. But we have discovered some things that allow us freedom and help us to keep family time a priority. Most important, especially now that our kids are teens, is planning Mass on Saturday evening or Sunday. Our approach has demanded flexibility, especially with Mom's work schedule. We often go together, but often we have to go separately, and we have learned the available Mass times throughout the area. Weekend planning is seasonal, and by that we usually mean sports seasons: soccer in the fall and spring, basketball and swimming in the winter. We've hinted above at how we think that sports schedules are becoming like an invasive species over family life; our response has been to engage moderately but to be ready to say no. We try to plan shared chores too so that everyone is working together. We hope to send the message that upkeep of our home is everyone's responsibility and that it is made light by everyone's contribution, no matter how small.

Does it always work, and is it always stress free? Hardly. But sometimes it does, and at the minimum, we see signs from time to time that at least everyone understands that family time includes the need to work together. It's not just about being entertained. Our hope, ultimately, is that planning weekends well allows for large spaces of leisure time to open up: time for spontaneity, time for relaxation, time that is not governed by the usual norms of necessity.

Questions for Discernment

1. We live in a world governed by the clock. The ancients did not; their time was governed more by the sun and moon, the seasons of the agricultural year, and the other cycles of nature. We easily lose our connection to nature in the modern, industrialized world. Do you make deliberate efforts to connect your children with the natural world? What

activities could you plan that would help them engage with the cycles of nature?

2. Liturgical time helps us to recover some of this sense of the rhythms of life. The Church's seasons grew out of ancient Israelite celebrations rooted in agriculture. Familiarize yourself with the Church's liturgical cycle—you can easily read about it online—and then consider ways to help your children understand and enter into these seasons more deliberately.

3. Family life benefits by not getting caught up in the clock, chronological time. We have the opportunity to live in kairos time, the "acceptable time" or "opportune time," every time our children ask for time with us, to play or just have fun together. It is delightful, if we allow ourselves that freedom. When have you experienced kairos with members of your family?

4. Kairos time affords us the opportunity to develop contemplation, for we no longer see the world as costing us time or money. We see it as an opportunity to encounter each other and to encounter the Lord. Do you sometimes fail to see the reality of God "right under your nose"? Do your children? How can you help your children see the world more intentionally through the lenses of grace or relationships?

5. Festivity is a kind of contemplation, for it is a withdrawal from usefulness and dwelling in a kind of kairos. Family life benefits from making a priority of festivity, which can be related to the various seasons as well as birthdays or other specific holidays. What are some opportunities your family has for festivity?

CHAPTER SIX

A Family Mission

Years ago, the management guru Peter Drucker was fond of pointing to an image, a kind of parable, that suggested what meaningful work looked like. We believe it can also teach us something about reclaiming family life by reminding us of the meaningfulness embedded in the daily life of our sacred calling. The image was of three stonecutters, all doing the same work, who were asked what they were doing. The first replied, "Making a living." The second replied, "Becoming the best stonecutter in the world." The third, though, paused and, with a faraway look, a smile on his face, and a gleam in his eye, said, "I'm building a cathedral." He continued for several minutes, describing what the cathedral would look like and how people would come to worship there.

As parents, our lives are similarly about cathedral building, in the sense that we undertake the daily work of creating beauty. And like the stonecutters, on many days the work is repetitive, tiring, and all-consuming. To be sure, some days we feel like the first one, slogging through our daily chores (often on little sleep). On other days, though, we may get the sense that we are doing something really well by raising our children the way we do. Perhaps it is a concert at which your daughter plays the flute and people remark how beautifully she played.

Or perhaps it's an award banquet at the end of the swimming season, when your son receives a rookie-of-the-year award, even though he only learned how to swim a year before. Or maybe it's your daughter bringing home a report card that shows remarkable progress from a year ago. You swell with pride, and for a moment you begin to see your daily labor as contributing to something great.

There is a darker side to the second stonecutter though, evidenced perhaps most vividly by the so-called mommy wars that make parenthood a kind of competition. Whose Facebook posts show the greatest creativity in making Halloween costumes? Who has given up the most to ensure that their children succeed in school? Whose kids make the honor roll, win the state championship, ace the SAT, or earn a scholarship to a great college? These markers of successful parenting make it seem as though we can live vicariously through our children, when really, it's all about our own pride.

Our call, as parents, is ultimately to be like the third stonecutter, reminding ourselves from time to time that what we are doing is participating in God's creative, beautiful work in creation itself. Commenting on Drucker's story, Harvard president Drew Faust points to what the third stonecutter is really doing, reminding us of the true meaning of our work:

This project aspires to the heavens, transcending the earthbound—and indeed transcending the timebound as well, for cathedrals are built not in months or even years, but over centuries. A lifetime of work may make only a small contribution to a structure that unites past and future, connects humans across generations and joins their efforts to purposes they see as far larger than themselves.[50]

It is very easy to get stuck in modes like that of the first stonecutter, especially during the busy "middle periods" of our lives—the middle of the school year, the middle of a busy day, the middle of our family's life. Raising children takes a long time, especially if there is a significant age gap between the oldest and the youngest: parenting children can take twenty, thirty, even forty years of our lives—and of course, parenting does not stop when our children are adults. Faust reminds us that having the long view of our family mission changes the way we see our daily work.

> What we desire for our family is really rather simple: connection.

Parenting, like cathedral building, aspires to the heavens. We are nurturing our children's lives. We are helping to dispose them to receive God's grace in freedom in order that they might use their talents to help build his kingdom and thereby achieve their happiness. Daily, that work involves many thousands of "stones"—making meals, encouraging reading, teaching fair play, directing chores, modeling good behavior, exhorting them to make good choices. Rarely, though, will this work feel like it is anywhere near the heavens, particularly in those early stages that involve intimate familiarity with messes. Yet from a theological perspective, that immersion in the mess of life is a reminder of Christ's Incarnation: it is the kind of mess that Mary and Joseph experienced too as they nurtured the early life of our Savior.

Like the work of the third stonecutter, the work of parenting spans the centuries, knitting together the various strands of a family's story. We suspect that this dimension of a family's mission is less easy to recall today compared to generations ago. For much of human history, families spent generations and generations rooted to a particular patch of earth where connection to the past was as easy as walking to the well dug by a distant ancestor. Even in more recent American history, tight-knit ethnic communities offered reminders of families' struggles to provide a better life for children and grandchildren. The first child to graduate from college offered a source of great pride for those elders who had braved wars and migrations to ensure a future for their families.

Today, though, the fragmentation and alienation that can result from geographic and economic mobility are great challenges to many families. Our families of origin, to use one example, are spread out across California, Illinois, Alabama, Georgia, Connecticut, and Massachusetts, making extended family gatherings rare and difficult. Moreover, we are raising children who are likely to have no opportunity to ever meet their birth parents, whose brave decisions to give them life and a future by placing them for adoption were the consequence, at least in part, of the economic conditions in their country of birth. For us and our children, our family story is impacted by the stories of generations that preceded us and by the social and political forces that have shaped both recent and more distant history.

Also, like the third stonecutter, our lives as parents are likely to be one part—however great or small—of the lives that our children ultimately come to live. As we reflect on the influence of our own parents growing up, we can point to specific ways that they have influenced and shaped us for good and not so good. Yet as any psychologist will tell you, the full impact of one's parents is often submerged, hidden from obvious reflection. The best we can do is try to parent mindfully: that is, with a discerning eye toward the great good that our children will inhabit as adults. We are not raising children, we are raising future men and women who will serve the world and who one day will take care of us in our old age.

The Schedule of Daily Life

We have suggested that reclaiming family life from overscheduling comes from keeping ourselves rooted in practices that keep us mindful of the big picture—the cathedral, to use our image above. Seeking and taking advantage of leisure time, centering our lives on worship, celebrating kairos times and seasons—all these keep our hearts close to the Lord. They allow us to be like trees planted near streams of life-giving water, as suggested by Jeremiah's rich image:

> They are like a tree planted beside the waters
>   that stretches out its roots to the stream:

It does not fear heat when it comes,
    its leaves stay green;
In the year of drought it shows no distress,
    but still produces fruit. (Jeremiah 17:8)

The image of being well rooted strikes us as helpful for considering the constantly pressing question: how much is too much? In our lives there are regular opportunities for ourselves and our kids, and so we must develop a discerning eye to judge the schedule of daily life.

Some kids are, without doubt, overscheduled. In recent years, there have been a number of books and essays addressing this concern. Consider the titles: *Pressured Parents, Stressed-Out Kids*; "Overscheduled Child May Lead to Bored Teen," "Overscheduled Children: How Big a Problem?" These and many others have taken a look at the effects of shuffling kids from one activity to the next, running them through various adult-designed programs and curricula—often for the sake of keeping kids occupied while parents are at work. Researchers raised concerns about the lack of truly free time in their lives and the lost opportunity for kids to develop imagination and relationship skills like negotiation and compassion.

Yet not long after this push to consider kids being overscheduled, there was pushback. Other researchers pointed out that outside activities can be great for kids, helping them to develop new skills and interests that they might not develop by engaging in spontaneous play among kids in the neighborhood or heading down to the old swimming hole. (By the way, what we've found is that these kinds of ideal play settings exist only in our imagination. Our kids' free time can tend toward the sedentary—playing video games, watching TV, and so on. The world they live in is not the one we grew up in. But that's a cultural analysis for a different book.)

Alvin Rosenfeld, a child and adolescent psychiatrist and one of the authors of *The Over-Scheduled Child*, puts overscheduling in perspective. According to him, the key is a balance of having good activities as well as good down time for both parents and kids, as well as time to come together for shared activities. The important message, he says, is that parents communicate the message that kids are cherished and loved in both scheduled and unscheduled time.[51]

> An important dimension of a family's mission is to make the nurturing of lifelong relationships central.

That counsel makes sense to us. But it may require some reminders from time to time, especially during periods when work is consuming and kids need a lot of attention. Too often, we think of what might make our lives feel more free. "If only we didn't have to go to soccer games every Saturday!" "If only Mom didn't have to go to work every Sunday morning!" "If only Dad didn't have to go on that work trip during vacation week!" We think of reclaiming family life in terms of negative freedom—that is, the ability to reach a better state by removing some problem. The challenge, we suggest, is to develop a more robust understanding of our positive freedom, defined as the capacity to make choices within the ordinary limitations of our lives that allow us to flourish as individuals and families.

Positive freedom is the ability to be happy in the everyday. It is rooted, we think, in the confidence that God has made us for a purpose and called us together as a family—a key theme we explore in our book *Six Sacred Rules for Families*. It is rooted in the desire to find grace in the ordinary, joy in the day-to-day, meaning in the stories of lives intertwined through the growing-up years. It is a quality of vision, more than a function of getting everything we want.

Consider a brief thought experiment. What would you do if you won the lottery? What if, in other words, your family life was no longer limited by financial concerns, and you had limitless freedom to choose the kind of lifestyle you thought best? Your life would be one of limitless leisure. Would you be happy?

Negative Freedom, Positive Freedom

Most people would, we think, say yes. But in fact, in studies done of people who have won the lottery and of others who have that kind of freedom, happiness seems rather elusive.[52] Those who have massive amounts of money and power, more-over, often suffer from a kind of depression rooted in an inability to decide what to do with themselves.[53] It may be enticing to dream about having the kind of freedom that would come with money and power, but what these studies suggest is that the issue is not that simple. The more important question, we suggest, has to do with what is worth desiring out of our lives. And for us who are parents, that question has another, richer dimension—it is the question of what to desire for our family life. Too often, we think of the answer to that question in the negative sense: what might we remove from our busy lives in order to feel happier? (Think, perhaps, about the time you spend driving kids to activities or helping with homework or other daily chores.) We certainly feel happier, for example, when summer comes and there's no morning routine of getting kids to school!

But the question has an altogether different angle to consider, approaching the question in a positive sense: once all those things you wished could be taken away were, in fact, taken away, what would you do as a family? How would you spend your time? What would you want to accomplish? What would you teach your kids? What stories would you want to tell? What stories would you want your kids to tell?

What we desire for our family is really rather simple: connection. We hope that times of spontaneity help our kids to understand the simple truth that we love to be around them and to do things together. Individual activities are good, to be sure. They help our kids to explore their talents, negotiate relationships with peers and adults, discover new dimensions to their personalities, get exercise, develop self-discipline, and many other goods. But beyond all these discrete goods that they experience in activities, we want to hold on to the priority of family life itself, for it is a positive good that gives rise to a litany of other goods. For only in the context of connecting with others can a child discover the key to happiness—that it's about the way we relate to those closest to us. The most extensive research study ever undertaken proves it.

The Seventy-Five-Year Harvard Study of Happiness

In 1938, Harvard researchers selected a group of undergraduate students and asked them to complete surveys about their lives: their physical and emotional well-being, their relationships, their life choices. (Among them was future U.S. president John F. Kennedy.) Eventually, the researchers also included a group of men from Dorchester, a working-class area of Boston, to compare them to the comparatively affluent cohort of Harvard men. For seventy-five years, these teams of researchers tracked every imaginable aspect of these men's lives to learn what they could about the factors that impact a person's happiness.

The fourth director of that study is Robert Waldinger, a psychiatrist and psychoanalyst whose TED talk (with over twelve million views as of this writing) summarized the findings of this epic study.[54] Summarizing the results, Waldinger writes, "Simply put, good relationships keep us happy and healthy." More than any other factor—health, wealth, power, or any other—the quality of a person's relationships impacted his or her happiness.

He asks an important question of individuals that could apply equally well to families: if you were to invest in your future best self, where would you put your time and energy? It's this question that suggests to us a direction for considering our family's mission. Is it to get our kids into college? To make them great athletes or musicians? Or is it about providing a regular habit of positive experiences? Or something else?

Our lives are not a series of disconnected moments, but loving creations of a God who is patient and who draws all things toward some good.

What we find in our experience is that it's very easy to get into a kind of autopilot when it comes to the question of mission. Go to work, go to school, go on vacation, rinse and repeat. Lacking a sense of mission, family time becomes caught up in whatever are the common patterns we see around us. But the common patterns, at least when we compare them to our own growing-up years, are increasingly fragmented, as we've suggested. The most obvious example to us is the encroachment on Sundays, a day that used to be free from scheduled activities (like sports) but now are days as packed as any other day. We faced the reality of this issue recently, when having to discern whether to sign one of our children up for a club sports team that practiced Sunday mornings—an experience necessary for becoming a captain on next year's squad. We resented having to decide between our family's usual worship time and our child's advancement on the team. (With our child, we decided to postpone involvement on the team till the summer, thereby preserving our Sundays.)

What the Harvard study points to is an important dimension of a family's mission: namely, to make the nurturing of lifelong relationships central. When we consider a lifetime of relationships—those people whom we will love decades from now—we reframe the importance of the daily interactions that comprise family life.

Children, of course, won't easily grasp the importance of this truth, but we find ourselves circling back to it again and again. Last year, to use one example, we were trying to plan a weekend away during a very busy and stressful stretch of time. We desperately wanted to reconnect with each other and with our kids, and so were delighted to find a couple of unplanned days that would allow us to do that. One of our kids, though, absolutely dug in her heels, refusing to go because there was a party at a friend's house that Friday night. From her perspective, it was an important social event and "everyone would be there." Our perspective was different. We needed the time together as a family during a summer that was quickly getting away from us. We stressed that times like these created memories that lasted for many years. And we tried to suggest—with very little success!—that the relationships with her family members were going to last far longer than the relationships with the group of people at the party, most of whom would be going to different schools in a year or two anyway.

Our daughter was not convinced by our arguments, and we did have to force her to come away with us, much to her displeasure. But we are certain that our logic was right: we needed to get away as a family and spend time together. Happily, her mood eventually relaxed and she did, in fact, enjoy the time away; we have some great memories of that trip. We were willing to go to the wall over the opportunity precisely because of the importance we attach to making our family relationships central to our lives, even during the difficult period of the teen years.

A Sense of Growth

In her book *The Happiness Project*, Gretchen Rubin describes a year when she "Spent a Year Trying to Sing in the Morning, Clean My Closets, Fight Right, Read Aristotle, and Generally Have More Fun."[55] Each month, she focused on one way to make her life happier and then analyzed the results of her efforts. And while she generated a number of useful insights, one general insight that has stuck with us is her conviction, consistent with Aristotle's philosophy, that a happy life involves a sense of growth. That insight resonates with what we've observed in our sixteen years of parenting: when we feel as though our efforts are yielding fruit, life feels better. When we see that our children are thriving, or that our work is building toward some greater good, we feel a sense of freshness and energy.

There are, we think, right and wrong ways of considering a sense of growth. Children are free creatures of God, and so attaching our too-narrow ideas of what constitutes success, as we've suggested, can be harmful. We do watch their grades and talk with them about the value of hard work, but we do not measure growth in exclusively academic terms. Primarily, our concern is how they are as persons, including the ways they engage in relationships with members of the family and with others. How do they talk to one another? Do they show signs of generosity? Do they play together? Can they joke around with us? What are signs of thoughtfulness they show—doing a chore without complaint, helping with homework, sharing food? Conversely, do they say mean things? Do they get caught up in their own worlds, like sequestering themselves in their rooms? Do they refuse to do normal chores?

None of these behaviors, positive or negative, are ever the final word. For us, the images of God's relentlessness—forgiving seventy times seven times, leaving the ninety-nine sheep behind in order to search for the lost one, waiting patiently for the prodigal son to return—these are images of the kind of long view we hope to take as parents.

As we suggested in the section dealing with festivity, times of celebration are opportune for recalling how life is from year to year. What are the differences we see this year compared to last? How have our children grown, not only physically but also emotionally, spiritually, or intellectually? How have we ourselves changed, based on life circumstances, relationships, or health? Placing all these concerns before God reminds us that our lives are not a series of disconnected moments, but loving creations of a God who is patient and who draws all things toward some good.

Paideia

To summarize our points in this chapter so far, we've suggested that our lives as parents are like the third stonecutter, energized by a vision of the beauty that our work helps build over the course of our lives. We can lose sight of that vision when our lives become too crowded with activity, even the many good opportunities we may offer our children over the course of their lives.

What we most deeply desire as human beings is connection. Members of our families are lifelong relationships that provide important sources of connection, and so it is important to prioritize the daily work of relationship building. Doing so, suggests the Harvard study, is the surest way to happiness. Further, our happiness is tied to a sense of growth, and we must take the long view in order to discern signs of authentic growth in our relationships with one another.

One way to conceive of our role as parents in the family is that we provide the long view. Children are incapable of fully understanding a life span or how their priorities today will be very different from their priorities ten years from now. As parents, our vision of our children moves between memory of who they once were, attention to who they are today, and hopes for the people they will become. Walking with them as we do, our concern is that they eventually learn to walk confidently on their own, taking advantage of every opportunity to teach them necessary life lessons along the way.

The Greek word *paideia* refers to the formation of young people for citizenship in society. With roots in thinkers such as Plato, Aristotle, and Isocrates, paideia involved not only intellectual development but also the cultivation of the virtues necessary for a young person to assume leadership. Today the term can refer to the vision of flourishing we hope to cultivate in our children. With such a vision, parents approach life with a mission that transforms all aspects of their shared lives and makes all times—chronos and kairos—fit for the family's mission.

> What is family life other than a series of building blocks, stones, that over time become a cathedral?

A recent example in our own lives reminds us of the way that the mission of paideia transforms a family's time. It was midwinter, the time of year when there are the highest reports of depression among the general population. Days are short, the weather in New England tends to be awful, and people can be testy and short-tempered. Over one weekend, there was a snowstorm: a fairly average one, dumping six or eight inches of snow on all the roadways. Activities were cancelled and people stayed indoors, waiting for the road crews to plow. For us, the storm was an opportunity: we wanted to make sure we had time to teach our daughter, who was learning how to drive, how to manage on snowy roads. We made some time after her work shift to practice braking in a parking lot, feeling the way that the antilock brakes engaged under these conditions. It was an opportune time.

Several observations are worth noting. First, we were not in particularly good moods, in part due to the weather and general exhaustion. Second, our daughter was tired from work and irritable. Had you taken a camera to film the way we related to each other, you would not have seen a family that had everything figured out perfectly. Nevertheless, as we reflect on the experience, what we see is the way that our mission of paideia—exemplified in this example as teaching our daughter a skill about driving in snowy conditions—transformed our ordinary experience of a dreary day.

Paideia means that we are vigilant about the way that ordinary life becomes a gift to another—another stone in a cathedral. It is a key to reclaiming any time as family time, because it is an attitude of readiness to make any experience one of connection, relationship, and learning. For what is family life other than a series of building blocks, stones, that over time become a cathedral? These stones vary over the years, and their shapes depend on what parents can teach and children can learn. Early on, they are simple things like learning to walk and talk. They are playtimes, reading together, walks in a carriage, and rides on the new tricycle. Eventually they are playdates with other children, learning to write and color, doing puzzles or building with blocks. Soon these stones are related to school, friends, activities outside the home, and eventually driving lessons, relationship advice, lessons about drugs and alcohol, and help with choosing a college.

So how might we reclaim family time? We seize opportunities for paideia: opportunities to share something of ourselves with our children, in the hope that it might contribute to their flourishing as persons. Any time can be an opportune time.

Questions for Discernment

Spend some time in prayer for each of your children. Ask yourself:

1. What significant challenges do our children currently face?

2. What areas of growth must they prioritize?

3. What talents or gifts must we help them cultivate?

4. Do they have an understanding of how their gifts might be used in service to others?

5. What relationships ought we help them to develop?

6. What are the major activities that take up their time?

7. Are they bored?

8. Do their activities help them to discern who God is calling them to be? Do they represent areas of growth in their lives?

9. Is there something missing from their lives?

10. Do they have a sense of their life's purpose?

11. What do we see as areas of their lives where they need help or where they need to be challenged?

12. How do they like to spend their free time?

13. Do we see them engaging in anything we consider corrosive or destructive of their character?

Epilogue

Love, and do what you will.
—St. Augustine

The Christian life is rooted in a desire to imitate Christ and a faith that doing so will allow us to grow ever closer to living the mission for which God has given us life in the first place. For those of us whom the Lord has called to parenthood, he has offered a life-giving approach to time, even when life is hard. For family life is by definition a life in communion; it is a life that can heal the pains of loneliness and orient our desires toward those we love.

There is, we suggest, a fundamental ethic of family life—namely, to grow in love for one another. "I give you a new commandment: love one another. As I have loved you, so you also should love one another. This is how all will know that you are my disciples, if you have love for one another" (John 13:34-35). These words that Jesus spoke to his disciples toward the end of his public ministry apply to us as well. Reclaiming family time is fundamentally about observing this commandment. And like all of the commandments, this one is about coming to realize our freedom.

In these final reflections, we'd like to focus on a question that faces all parents in different ways over the life cycle: "What about some me time?" If the Lord commands us to love one another, does that mean that we must always spend our time with family? The short answer: of course not.

Recall that at various points during his public ministry, Jesus took time away by himself in prayer (Matthew 14:13; Luke 5:16; 22:41; John 6:15) and even expressed exasperation and anger at the people around him (Mark 9:19; John 2:14-16). If Jesus found the need to take time away from people who could sometimes drive him crazy, so can we. The commandment to love is not a call to an unrealistic messiah complex—even for Jesus—but rather a call to live within the reality of the persons that the Lord has created us to be.

Recall, too, that in the chapter on leisure, we explored the ancient idea that it is about taking time to nourish the soul. All people need forms of leisure, however basic. At the various stages of a family's life cycle, different forms of leisure emerge. We can recall moments during our daughters' early years when a cup of coffee during their naps or a quick run to the gym before anyone woke up provided a needed opportunity to recharge our batteries. Later, as our kids got older, perhaps it was a night out with friends or a day retreat. Experiences like these are reminders of how fluid time can be. An hour with a friend may leave a more lasting impression than eight hours of work.

There is a legal rule that applies in a different way to family ways: *nemo dat quod non habet* (no one gives what he does not have). You can't teach your children how to take care of themselves if you do not model the same for yourself. Reclaiming family time is not about making sure that your children are entertained every second of the day, nor is it about insisting that all activities be done as a family. It is about something more fundamental, something rooted in a vision of the eternal. Let us explain.

> If the Lord commands us to love one another, does that mean that we must always spend our time with family?

There is a paradox in family life: it is an all-encompassing, total commitment of life, and yet it changes and eventually slips away. The harried mother of babies and the sleep-deprived father of toddlers become the busy, strategizing parents of school-age children. Over time, they have older children, teens, young adults, sons- or daughters-in-law, grandchildren. Each stage of the family life cycle is different, and each year brings new challenges. Family patterns change, new challenges arise, and children develop personalities with attendant likes and dislikes. Our challenge is to develop practices of prayer and self-awareness through these changes, mindful that over time, children will become adults with their own lives and relationships.

Family time does not end; in some ways it becomes more precious because it becomes more rare. We were mindful of that truth recently when both of us had such rare experiences to be with all of our siblings and parents. As we've said, our families of origin are now spread across the United States, and so reunions are very special occasions. They are fruits of the investments in family time that we ourselves experienced as young people and represent for us hopes for our children as they get older.

Family adds richness to life, but the flow of life is such that we cannot live exclusively as though our children or spouses are the only worthy recipients of our time and attention. Taking time for ourselves is part of making a priority of family life. It is part of the commandment to love one another, because it is rooted in the faith that love is ultimately a gift of God that we must carefully cultivate in ourselves and in our relationships.

Over time, the practice of living contemplatively allows us to discern the beauty in ordinary life and to enjoy the gifts that our family members bring—even if they are sometimes frustrating! If contemplation is a "long loving look at the real," then contemplation of our family life is a long loving look at each other and ourselves.

> You can't teach your children how to take care of themselves if you do not model the same for yourself.

We live richly in the memories of past experiences, the appreciation of present experiences, and the hope of future experiences. That is really the essence of reclaiming family time. It is not only about carving time out of the calendar or careful planning of time away. It is rather about bringing a discerning attitude to daily life. "This is the day the LORD has made; / let us rejoice in it and be glad" (Psalm 118:24). Our family prayer, then, is this. What is yours?

Lord, we thank you for the gift of our family.

We are grateful for your calling us together to be shelter for each other.

We pray for the grace to see you in each other's face and to show each other your love every day.

Stay with us always, and guide us in our choices so that we may walk with you in the building of your kingdom. Amen!

Notes

1. Seth Maxon, "How Sleep Deprivation Decays the Mind and Body," *The Atlantic*, December 30, 2013.

2. Kate Moriarty, "What We've Learned about Kids and Sleep in 2015," *Huffington Post*, September 9, 2015.

3. On homework, see Katie Reilly, "Is Homework Good for Kids? Here's What the Research Says," *Time*, August 30, 2016.

4. Bruce Feiler, "Overscheduled Children: How Big a Problem?" *New York Times*, October 11, 2013.

5. See Bureau of Labor Statistics, "Employment Characteristics of Families Summary," https://www.bls.gov/news.release/famee.nr0.htm.

6. Brigid Schulte, *Overwhelmed: Work, Love, and Play When No One Has the Time* (New York: Sarah Crichton Books, 2014).

7. Ibid, 30.

8. Ibid, 34.

9. See Emma Gray, "A Record Percentage of Women Don't Have Kids. Here's Why That Makes Sense," *Huffington Post*, April 9, 2015, http://www.huffingtonpost.com/2015/04/09/childless-more-women-are-not-having-kids-says-census_n_7032258.html.

10. See, for example, Jenna Goudreau, "The 10 Best Jobs for Work and Family Balance," *Forbes,* December 12, 2012, http://www.forbes.com/sites/jennagoudreau/2012/12/12/the -10-best-jobs-for-work-and-family-balance/#2551773c56d6.

11. One example is Boston College's Center for Work and Family, www.bc.edu/centers/cwf/.

12. Michael Pratt outlines these various approaches in his essay "The Power of Addressing the 'Why': Catholic Education as a Source of Meaningfulness and Competitive Advantage," *Integritas* 7.3 (Spring 2016), 1–16.

13. Schulte, 39.

14. Schulte, 35.

15. See Thomas Baker, "The Decline of Catholic Marriages," *Commonweal,* July 15, 2015, www.common -wealmagazine.org/decline-catholic-marriages.

16. Fredrick Buechner, *The Sacred Journey* (San Francisco: HarperOne, reprint 1991), 9–10.

17. See Genesis 3:17-19, in which the punishment for disobeying God includes having to work the earth in order to eat.

18. Jesus, in speaking of himself as the good shepherd, says, "I came so that they might have life and have it more abundantly."

19. See the *Catechism of the Catholic Church,* 2205 and 2204; see also Vatican II, *Lumen Gentium* (Dogmatic

Constitution on the Church), 11, and Pope St. John Paul II, *Familiaris Consortio* (The Role of the Christian Family in the Modern World), 21.

20. *Catechism of the Catholic Church*, 2207.

21. For more on discernment in family life, see our book *The Discerning Parent: An Ignatian Guide to Raising Your Teen* (Notre Dame, IN: Ave Maria Press, 2017).

22. See our book *Six Sacred Rules for Families* (Notre Dame, IN: Ave Maria Press, 2013) for more on the Examen in family life.

23. William McNamara as quoted by Walter J. Burghardt, SJ, "Contemplation: A Long Loving Look at the Real," *Church*, no. 5 (Winter 1989), 14–17.

24. Dante, *Purgatorio*, Canto 10.

25. Augustine, *City of God*, book 19, chapter 19, in Gerald G. Walsh, SJ, and Daniel J. Honan, trans., *The Fathers of the Church: Saint Augustine*, The City of God, *Books XVII–XXII* (Washington, DC: Catholic University of America Press, 2008), 230.

26. Aristotle, *Politics*, book 10, chapter 7.

27. Josef Pieper, *Leisure: The Basis of Culture*, trans. Alexander Dru (New York: Pantheon Books, 1952, 1964).

28. Ibid, 48.

29. Ibid, 30.

30. Evagrius Ponticus describes the "eight thoughts" that get in the way of growth in the spiritual life in his work *Praktikos*. Of acedia, he writes, "The demon of acedia . . . drives [the monk] to desire other sites where he can more easily procure life's necessities, more readily find work and make a real success of himself." See Harvey D. Egan, *An Anthology of Christian Mysticism* (Collegeville, MN: Liturgical Press, 1996), 49.

31. Justin Martyr, I Apology 67: *Patrologia Graeca* 6, 429 and 432; cited in the *Catechism of the Catholic Church*, 2174.

32. Quoted in Michael Himes, "Living Conversation: Higher Education in a Catholic Context," in *An Ignatian Spirituality Reader*, ed. George Traub (Chicago: Loyola Press, 2008), 237.

33. *Catechism of the Catholic Church*, 2172; Exodus 31:17; cf. 23:12. Cf. Nehemiah 13:15-22; 2 Chronicles 36:21.

34. Bonnie Thurston, *To Everything a Season: A Spirituality of Time* (Eugene, OR: Wipf and Stock, 1999), 107.

35. See Matthew 9:24; 12:15; 14:13; and 15:21.

36. See our book *The Discerning Parent* (Notre Dame, IN: Ave Maria Press, 2017) for more on discernment in family life.

37. Pieper, 18, citing Thomas Aquinas, *Summa Theologica* II.ii.141, 5 ad 1.

38. See the *Catechism of the Catholic Church*, 2042.

39. Quoted in Esther de Waal, *A Seven Day Journey with Thomas Merton* (Guilford, Surrey, England: Eagle, 1992), 43.

40. This is the explanation given in Liddell and Scott's Greek-English lexicon.

41. Cicero, *De natura deorum*, II.xxv.

42. Matthew, Mark, and Luke present the story as happening at Passover, but John presents it as happening right before Passover.

43. Compare Isaiah 6:9-10; John 9:39; 12:40; Acts 28:26-27; and Romans 11:8, to name a few.

44. Ernst Jünger, *Blätter und Steine* (Leaves and Stones), 202 (1934), cited in Pieper, 9.

45. Thomas Aquinas, *Summa Theologica* I-II, q. 3, a. 5.

46. Aquinas, *Summa Theologica*, III, q. 40, a. 1, ad 2. See also Marie-Dominique Chenu, *Aquinas and His Role in Theology* (Collegeville, MN: Liturgical Press, 2002), 46.

47. St. Ignatius writes, "God works and labors for me in all things created on the face of the earth—that is, behaves like one who labors—as in the heavens, elements, plants, fruits, cattle, etc., giving them being, preserving them, giving them vegetation and sensation, etc." *Spiritual Exercises*, "Contemplation to attain divine love," third point.

48. See Walter Burghardt, SJ, "Contemplation: A Long Loving Look at the Real," reprinted in George W. Traub, SJ, *An Ignatian Spirituality Reader* (Chicago: Loyola Press, 2008), 89–98.

49. Sirach 30:22. Compare Fyodor Dostoevsky, *The Brothers Karamazov*, book 7, chapter 4: "He has made Himself like unto us from love and rejoices with us. He is changing the water into wine that the gladness of the guests may not be cut short." (Translated by Constance Garnett.)

50. Quoted in "Three Stonecutters: On the Future of Business Education," *Harvard Business Magazine*, October 15, 2008, at http://harvardmagazine.com/breaking-news/three-stonecutters-the-future-business-education.

51. Alvin Rosenfeld, as cited in Feiler, "Overscheduled Children: How Big a Problem?"

52. See Melissa Dahl, "A Classic Psychology Study on Why Winning the Lottery Won't Make You Happier," *New York Magazine*, January 13, 2016, http://nymag.com/scienceofus/2016/01/classic-study-on-happiness-and-the-lottery.html. The theory is that major change only shifts the emotional baseline so that it becomes the new normal and hence the new boring.

53. See Alice G. Walton, "Why the Super-Successful Get Depressed," *Forbes* January 26, 2015, http://www.forbes.com/sites/alicegwalton/2015/01/26/why-the-super-successful-get-depressed/#3562d4c82b1a.

54. See Robert Waldinger's website, including a link to his TED talk, at http://robertwaldinger.com/about/.

55. Gretchen Rubin, *The Happiness Project: Or, Why I Spent a Year Trying to Sing in the Morning, Clean My Closets, Fight Right, Read Aristotle, and Generally Have More Fun* (New York: HarperCollins, revised edition, 2015).

the WORD
among us®
The *Spirit* of Catholic Living

This book was published by The Word Among Us. Since 1981, The Word Among Us has been answering the call of the Second Vatican Council to help Catholic laypeople encounter Christ in the Scriptures.

The name of our company comes from the prologue to the Gospel of John and reflects the vision and purpose of all of our publications: to be an instrument of the Spirit, whose desire is to manifest Jesus' presence in and to the children of God. In this way, we hope to contribute to the Church's ongoing mission of proclaiming the gospel to the world so that all people would know the love and mercy of our Lord and grow more deeply in their faith as missionary disciples.

Our monthly devotional magazine, *The Word Among Us*, features meditations on the daily and Sunday Mass readings and currently reaches more than one million Catholics in North America and another half million Catholics in one hundred countries around the world. Our book division, The Word Among Us Press, publishes numerous books, Bible studies, and pamphlets that help Catholics grow in their faith.

To learn more about who we are and what we publish, log on to our website at www.wau.org. There you will find a variety of Catholic resources that will help you grow in your faith.

Embrace His Word, Listen to God . . .

www.wau.org